EXCEL EXERCISES FOR TECHNICIAN

For Skills Tests in December 2005 and June 2006

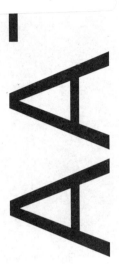

Workbook (with Excel files on CD)

In this April 2005 edition

- Layout designed to be easy on the eye – and easy to use

- Clear language and presentation

- Practical exercises - with data supplied on CD-ROM for use with Microsoft Excel

BPP
PROFESSIONAL EDUCATION

First edition May 2003
Third edition April 2005

ISBN 0 7517 2276 6 (previous edition 7517 1616 2)

British Library Cataloguing-in-Publication Data
A catalogue record for this book
is available from the British Library

Published by

BPP Professional Education
Aldine House, Aldine Place
London W12 8AW

www.bpp.com

Printed in Great Britain by WM Print
Frederick Street
Walsall
West Midlands
WS2 9NE

We are grateful to the Lead Body for Accounting for
permission to reproduce extracts from the Standards
of Competence for Accounting, and to the AAT for
permission to reproduce extracts from the mapping
and Guidance Notes.

Contents

Introduction

How to use this Workbook and CD-ROM – Using the Excel files provided on the CD – Information Technology and the AAT Standards of Competence – Building your portfolio

> Practice activities are short activities designed to help you acquire Excel skills relevant to the Standards of Competence.

> Assignments are designed to enable you to apply your Excel skills in realistic situations.

Order form

Review form & free prize draw

Introduction

How to use this Workbook and CD-ROM

Aims of this Workbook and CD-ROM

> To provide practice in Microsoft Excel skills relevant to your accounting work and to enable you to meet the AAT Standards of Competence.

> To tie in with the other components of the BPP Effective Study Package to ensure you have the best possible chance of success.

This Workbook

Qualifying as an Accounting Technician requires you to provide evidence of your practical computing skills.

This book contains a range of activities and assignments designed to help AAT students become proficient in the use of Microsoft Excel. Some knowledge of accounting and of Microsoft Excel is presumed. The level of prior knowledge required is that covered at AAT Foundation Level.

Interactive Texts and Practice and Revision Kits

Computer skills and computerised systems are relevant in Foundation Units 1-4 and Unit 21; Intermediate Unit 7; and Technician Units 8, 9, 10, 15 and 17. To ensure you have the knowledge you need for your assessments, ensure you study the relevant BPP Interactive Texts and Revision Kits for these units. This Workbook and CD-ROM provides additional, practical knowledge and examples.

Passcards

These short memorable notes are focused on key topics, designed to remind you of what the Interactive Text has taught you.

Using the Excel files provided on the CD

The CD-ROM that accompanies this book contains data that you will need to complete some of Activities and Assignments. Spreadsheet data is provided in **Microsoft Excel** format.

To make use of this data **you need:**

- A CD-ROM drive
- Microsoft Windows 95/98/ME/XP or Windows NT/2000
- Microsoft Excel 97 or a subsequent version

Installation

The data held on the CD needs to be installed on your computer's hard disk. Follow the instructions below.

Either...

From the taskbar click on **Start** and select **Run.** In the pop-up box type **D:\BPPTECH** and click **OK.** (This assumes your CD-ROM drive is drive D, if your CD-ROM drive has been assigned a different letter use that.)

Or...

View the CD-ROM in Windows Explorer and **double-click** on the **BPPTECH.exe** file.

You should then see the following pop-up box.

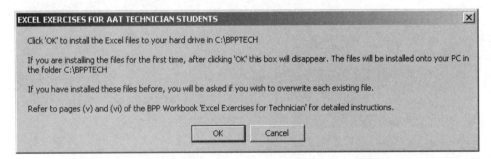

Click on **OK** in this pop-up box. If this is the first time you have installed the files, you don't need to do anything else. The Excel spreadsheet files will be installed on your hard disk in **C:\BPPTECH**. Refer to the 'What next?' section on the following page.

File already exists

If you see a message like the one below, the data has **already been installed** on your computer.

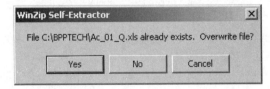

Click **Yes** to overwrite each file named in the box with a new version. Click **No** if you want to keep your current version of the file (for instance if you have made changes to it but saved it under its original name). New files that you have created with different names will not be affected.

What next?

If you have followed the instructions above the data has been copied into a folder on your hard drive called **C:\BPPTECH**. (You may need to press the **F5** key to refresh your screen before you can see this folder in Windows Explorer.)

If you double-click on this folder from within Windows Explorer you will find that it contains 30 spreadsheet files in **Microsoft Excel** format.

> **You will be told when and how to use each of these files when working through this book.**

Opening and saving the files

If you make any changes to the files provided by BPP you should **save** your modified file with a **new name**. That way you keep both a clean copy of the original and your own modified file.

If you accidentally modify a BPP file and then want a fresh copy of the original you can get one by **reinstalling** the data from the CD.

Information Technology and the AAT Standards of Competence

Under the Standards of Competence students are expected to demonstrate competence in the use of Information Technology (IT) throughout all three levels of the qualification.

Specific requirements are contained in Units 1-4, 7, 8, 9, 10, 15, 17 and 21. The basic requirements of the Standards are covered in the appropriate BPP Texts and Kits for these Units. Additional practical exercises relevant to Foundation Level are provided in the BPP Workbook 'Foundation Bookkeeping with Sage and Spreadsheets with Excel'.

This Workbook and CD is designed to provide additional practice in the use of Microsoft Excel relevant to Intermediate and Technician Levels.

Assessment

Units that include an IT element are examined using a variety of means including Skills Tests (Units 1, 2, 3, 4, 7, 21 Exams (3, 8 and 9) and a Project (10). Refer to the individual standards (reproduced in the relevant BPP Texts and Kits) for the details relating to individual units.

Where the Approved Assessment Centre is a **college or training organisation**, assessment will be by means of a combination of the following.

(a) Documentary evidence of activities carried out at the workplace, collected by you in an **accounting portfolio**

(b) Realistic **simulations** of workplace activities; these simulations may take the form of case studies and in-tray exercises and involve the use of primary documents and reference sources

(c) **Projects** and **assignments** designed to assess the Standards of Competence

If you are unable to provide workplace evidence, you will be able to complete the assessment requirements by the alternative methods listed above.

Computer related evidence in the portfolio relating to the Foundation Units may be distributed through the various units or may be filed in the Unit 21 section. Either way, the use of cross-referencing in the portfolio will be of paramount importance.

Building your portfolio

What is a portfolio?

A portfolio is a collection of work that demonstrates what the owner can do. In AAT language the portfolio demonstrates **competence**.

A painter will have a collection of his paintings to exhibit in a gallery, an advertising executive will have a range of advertisements and ideas that she has produced to show to a prospective client. Both the collection of paintings and the advertisements form the portfolio of that artist or advertising executive.

Your portfolio will be unique to you just as the portfolio of the artist will be unique because no one will paint the same range of pictures in the same way. It is a very personal collection of your work and should be treated as a **confidential** record.

What evidence should a portfolio include?

No two portfolios will be the same but by following some simple guidelines you can decide which of the following suggestions will be appropriate in your case.

(a) **Your current CV**

This should be at the front. It will give your personal details as well as brief descriptions of posts you have held with the most recent one shown first.

(b) **References and testimonials**

References from previous employers may be included especially those of which you are particularly proud.

(c) **Your current job description**

You should emphasise financial **responsibilities and duties**.

(d) **Your student record sheets**

These should be supplied by AAT when you begin your studies, and your training provider should also have some if necessary.

(e) **Evidence from your current workplace**

This could take many forms including **letters, memos, reports** you have written, **copies of accounts** or **reconciliations** you have prepared, **discrepancies** you have investigated etc. Remember to obtain permission to include the evidence from your line manager because some records may be sensitive. Discuss the performance criteria that are listed in your Student Record Sheets with your training provider and employer, and think of other evidence that could be appropriate to you.

(f) **Evidence from your social activities**

For example you may be the treasurer of a club in which case examples of your cash and banking records could be appropriate.

(g) **Evidence from your studies**

Few students are able to satisfy all the requirements of competence by workplace evidence alone. They therefore rely on simulations to provide the remaining evidence to complete a unit. If you are not working or not working in a relevant post, then you may need to rely more heavily on simulations as a source of evidence.

(h) **Additional work**

Your training provider may give you work that specifically targets one or a group of performance criteria in order to complete a unit. It could take the form of questions, presentations or demonstrations. Each training provider will approach this in a different way.

(i) **Evidence from a previous workplace**

This evidence may be difficult to obtain and should be used with caution because it must satisfy the 'rules' of evidence, that is, it must be current. Only rely on this as evidence if you have changed jobs recently.

(j) **Prior achievements**

For example you may have already completed the health and safety unit during a previous course of study, and therefore there is no need to repeat this work. Advise your training provider who will check to ensure that it is the same unit and record it as complete if appropriate.

How should it be presented?

As you assemble the evidence remember to **make a note** of it on your Student Record Sheet in the space provided and **cross reference** it. In this way it is easy to check to see if your evidence is **appropriate**. Remember one piece of evidence may satisfy a number of performance criteria so remember to check this thoroughly and discuss it with your training provider if in doubt. Keep all your evidence together in a ring binder or lever arch file for safe storage.

When should evidence be assembled?

You should begin to assemble evidence **as soon as you have registered as a student**. **Don't leave it all** until the last few weeks of your studies, because you may miss vital deadlines and your resulting certificate sent by the AAT may not include all the units you have completed. Give yourself and your training provider time to examine your portfolio and report your results to AAT at regular intervals. In this way the task of assembling the portfolio will be spread out over a longer period of time and will be presented in a more professional manner.

What are the key criteria that the portfolio must fulfil?

As you assemble your evidence bear in mind that it must be:

- **Valid**. It must relate to the Standards.
- **Authentic**. It must be your own work.
- **Current**. It must refer to your current or most recent job.
- **Sufficient**. It must meet all the performance criteria by the time you have completed your portfolio.

Finally

Remember that the portfolio is **your property** and **your responsibility**. Not only could it be presented to the external verifier before your award can be confirmed; it could be used when you are seeking **promotion** or applying for a more senior and better paid post elsewhere. How your portfolio is presented can say as much about you as the evidence inside.

For further information about portfolios, BPP have produced a book *Building Your Portfolio*. It can be ordered using the order form at the back of this book or at *www.bpp.com/aat*.

P A R T   A

Spreadsheets

Excel skills

Contents

Knowledge and understanding

4   Use of relevant computer packages

5   Methods of presenting information in graphical, diagrammatic and tabular form

The Unit Commentary for Unit 8 requires knowledge of how computer spreadsheets can assist you in preparing cost and performance information.

The Unit Commentary for Unit 9 requires knowledge of how computer spreadsheets can assist you in developing forecasts and budgets.

Other material relevant to the topic 'computer software' appears in BPP Texts/Kits for Units 4, 7, 8 and 9. The material in this book adds to the material produced for these Units.

1 Introduction

Spreadsheet skills are essential for people working in an accounting environment as much of the information produced in an accounting context is analysed or presented using spreadsheet software. This is reflected in the AAT Standards, which refer to spreadsheet skills at all Levels of the AAT qualification.

The exercises in *'Excel Exercises for Technician'* are designed for AAT students who **already possess basic Excel skills**. For example, the basic spreadsheet **construction** and **formatting** skills taught at Foundation Level are just as important at Intermediate and Technician Levels. These skills aren't covered in this book, as they are covered in the appropriate Texts and Kits, and in the BPP publication *'Foundation Bookkeeping with Sage and Spreadsheets with Excel'*.

2 Spreadsheet formulae

We start this book with a brief recap of some **basic spreadsheet formulae**.

2.1 Formula bar

The following illustration shows the formula bar. If the Formula bar is not visible when you open a spreadsheet choose **View**, **Formula bar** from the Excel main menu.

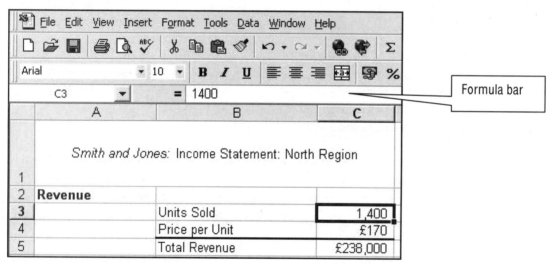

The formula bar allows you to see and edit the contents of the active cell. The bar also shows the cell address of the active cell (C3 in the example above).

2.2 Examples of spreadsheet formulae

Formulas in Microsoft Excel always start with an equals sign =. This is followed by the elements to be calculated (the operands) and the calculation operators. Each operand can be a value that does not change (a constant value), a cell or range reference, a label, a name, or a worksheet function.

Formulae can be used to perform a variety of calculations. Here are some examples.

(a) =C4*5. This formula **multiplies** the value in C4 by 5. The result will appear in the cell holding the formula.

(b) =C4*B10. This **multiplies** the value in C4 by the value in B10.

(c) =C4/E5. This **divides** the value in C4 by the value in E5. (* means multiply and / means divide by.)

(d) =C4*B10-D1. This **multiplies** the value in C4 by that in B10 and then subtracts the value in D1 from the result. Excel will perform multiplication and division before addition or subtraction. If in any doubt, use brackets (parentheses): =(C4*B10)–D1.

(e) =C4*117.5%. This **multiplies** the value in C4 by 1.175. This has the effect of adding 17.5% to the value in C4. This formula could be used to add 17.5% VAT to the value in C4.

(f) =(C4+C5+C6)/3. The **brackets** in this formula mean Excel would perform the addition first. Without the brackets, Excel would have first divided the value in C6 by 3, and then added the values in C4 and C5 to this.

(g) =2^2 gives you 2 **to the power** of 2, in other words 2^2 or 2 times 2. Likewise =2^3 gives you 2 cubed or 2^3 or 2 times 2 times 2.

(h) =4^(1/2) gives you the **square root** of 4. Likewise 27^(1/3) gives you the cube root of 27 and so on.

Excel calculates a formula from left to right. You can control how calculation is performed by changing the syntax of the formula. For example, the formula =5+2*3 gives a result of 11 because Excel calculates multiplication before addition. Excel would multiply 2 by 3 (resulting in 6) and would then add 5. You may use parentheses to change the order of operations. For example =(5+2)*3 would result in Excel firstly adding the 5 and 2 together, then multiplying that result by 3 to give 21.

2.3 Relative and Absolute Cell references

We will explain this concept by using an example. Formulae in 'standard' form, for example the formula =SUM(B7:B9) located in cell B10, are said to be **relative**. This formula does not really mean 'add up the numbers in cells B7 to B9'; it actually means 'add up the numbers in the three cells above this one'. So, if this relative formula was copied to cell C15 it would become =SUM(C12:C14). Sometimes this automatic amendment to copied formulae may not be required. In this situation you should use absolute referencing.

If we insert a dollar sign $ before the column letter, this makes the **column** reference **absolute**. So, copying =(SUM$B7:$B9) from B10 to C15 would give =SUM($B12:$B14).

A dollar sign before the row number makes the **row** number **absolute**. So, copying =(SUMB$7:B$9) from B10 to C15 would give =SUM(C$7:C$9).

A dollar sign before the column letter and row number makes the **complete cell reference absolute**. So, copying =(SUM$B$7:$B$9) from B10 to C15 would give =(SUM$B$7:$B$9).

You do not need to type the dollar signs, you can highlight the cell references you wish to make absolute and then press F4. This adds dollar signs to cell references in the formula, for example C31 would become $C$31. If you pressed F4 again, the reference becomes C$31. Press it again: the reference becomes $C31. Press it once more, and the simple relative reference is restored: C31.

2.4 Formulae with conditions

You should be familiar with simple spreadsheet formulae such as addition, subtraction, multiplication and division. Spreadsheets offer a range of more complex functions and formulae. You should experiment with these yourself – searching the word 'function' in Excel's Help facility is a good starting point. We will now look at an example of conditional formulae using an **IF statement**.

The following spreadsheet has been set up showing the difference between actual sales and target sales for four salesmen, and expressing the difference as a percentage of target sales.

	A	B	C	D	E	F
1	*Sales team comparison of actual against budget sales*					
2	Name	Sales (Budget)	Sales (Actual)	Difference	% of budget	
3		£	£	£	£	
4	Northington	275,000	284,000	9,000	3.27	
5	Souther	200,000	193,000	(7,000)	(3.50)	
6	Weston	10,000	12,000	2,000	20.00	
7	Easterman	153,000	152,000	(1,000)	(0.65)	
8						
9	Total	638,000	641,000	3,000	0.47	
10						

Suppose the company employing the salesmen in this example awards a bonus to those salesmen who exceed their target by more than £1,000. A formula could be entered into the spreadsheet to show who is entitled to the bonus. To do this we would enter the appropriate formula in cells F4 to F7. For salesperson Easterman, we would enter the following in cell F7: **=IF(D4>1000,"BONUS"," ")**

IF statements follow the following structure (or syntax). **=IF(logical_test,value_if_true,value_if_false)**

The logical_test is any value or expression that can be evaluated to Yes or No. For example, D4>1000 is a logical expression; if the value in cell D4 is over 1000, the expression evaluates to Yes. Otherwise, the expression evaluates to No.

Value_if_true is the value that is returned if the answer to the logical_test is Yes. For example, if the answer to D4>1000 is Yes, and the value_if_true is the text string "BONUS", then the cell containing the IF function will display the text "BONUS".

Value_if_false is the value that is returned if the answer to the logical_test is No. For example, if the value_if_false is two sets of quote marks "" this means display a blank cell if the answer to the logical test is No. So in our example, if D4 is not over 1000, then the cell containing the IF function will display a blank cell.

Note the following symbols which can be used in formulae with conditions:

<	less than (like L (for 'less') on its side)
<=	less than or equal to
=	equal to
>=	greater than or equal to
>	greater than
<>	not equal to

Care is required to ensure **brackets** and **commas** are entered in the right places. If, when you try out this kind of formula, you get an error message, it may well be a simple mistake, such as leaving a comma out.

2.4.1 Examples: formulae with conditions

A company offers a discount of 5% to customers who order more than £1,000 worth of goods. A spreadsheet showing what customers will pay might look like this.

	A	B	C	D	E	F
1	Discount Traders Ltd					
2	*Sales analysis – April 200X*					
3	Customer	Sales	5% discount	Sales (net)		
4		£	£	£		
5	Arthur	956.00	0.00	956.00		
6	Dent	1423.00	71.15	1351.85		
7	Ford	2894.00	144.70	2749.30		
8	Prefect	842.00	0.00	842.00		
9						
10						

The formula in cell C5 is: =IF(B5>1,000,(0.05*B5),0). This means, if the value in B5 is greater than £1,000 multiply it by 0.05, otherwise the discount will be zero. Cell D5 will calculate the amount net of discount, using the formula: =B5-C5. The same conditional formula with the cell references changed will be found in cells C6, C7 and C8. **Strictly**, the variables £1,000 and 5% should be entered in a **different part** of the spreadsheet.

Here is another example. Suppose the pass mark for an examination is 50%. You have a spreadsheet containing candidate's scores in column B. If a score is held in cell B10, an appropriate formula for cell C10 would be:

=IF(B10<50,"FAILED","PASSED").

3 More formulae and functions

In this section we shall have a quick look at some functions that are useful when you are presented with pre-prepared data in a spreadsheet and you want to extract certain items.

3.1 Left, right, mid and &

Sometimes you may want to extract only specific characters from the data entered in a cell. For instance, suppose a set of raw materials codes had been entered into a spreadsheet as follows.

	A	B
1	6589D	
2	5589B	
3	5074D	
4	8921B	
5	3827B	
6	1666D	
7	5062A	
8	7121D	
9	7457C	
10	9817D	
11	6390C	
12	1148A	
13	4103A	
14	8988A	
15	6547C	
16	5390A	
17	6189D	
18	8331C	
19	1992B	
20	7587A	

The four **digits** are, say, a number derived from the supplier's reference number, while the **letter** indicates that the material is used to make Product A, B, C or D.

If you wanted to sort this data in **alphabetical** order of **Product** you would have a problem, because it is only possible to arrange it in ascending or descending **numerical** order, using the standard Sort method.

As a work around for this problem, you could extract the letter from each cell using the **RIGHT** function, as follows.

	A	B
1	6589D	=RIGHT(A1,1)
2	5589B	=RIGHT(A2,1)
3	5074D	=RIGHT(A3,1)
4	8921B	=RIGHT(A4,1)
5	3827B	=RIGHT(A5,1)
6	1666D	=RIGHT(A6,1)

The formula in cell B1 means 'Extract the last (or rightmost) one character from cell A1'. If we wanted to extract the last **two** characters the formula would be **=RIGHT(A1,2)**, and so on. The formula can then be filled down, and we could then sort columns A and B 'by' column B, giving the following results.

	A	B
1	5062A	A
2	1148A	A
3	4103A	A
4	8988A	A
5	5390A	A
6	7587A	A
7	5589B	B
8	8921B	B
9	3827B	B
10	1992B	B
11	7457C	C
12	6390C	C
13	6547C	C
14	8331C	C
15	6589D	D
16	5074D	D
17	1666D	D
18	7121D	D
19	9817D	D
20	6189D	D

The function **LEFT** works in the same way, except that it extracts the **first** (or leftmost) character or characters.

The function **MID**, as you might expect, extracts a character or characters from the **middle** of the cell, starting at the **position** you specify, counting from left to right:

=MID([Cell],[Position],[Number of characters]).

In Excel the first character extracted is the one at the position specified, so if you want to extract the **third** character you specify position 3.

A similar function is the **Merge** function, which uses the & sign. Suppose data had been entered into columns A, B and C as shown below. In column D, you wish to combine all characters from A, B and C. The formula shown in cell D1 will do just that. The formula could be filled down to give the same results for the rest of the list.

	A	B	C	D
1	21	A	64	=A1&B1&C1
2	62	P	14	
3	87	T	26	
4				

3.2 Lookup

The LOOKUP function allows you to enter data that corresponds to a value in one cell in a column and return the data in the corresponding row in a different column. A simple example will make this clearer.

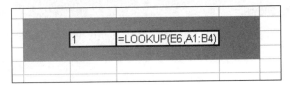

The user enters a figure between 1 and 4 in cell E6 and the spreadsheet returns the corresponding colour from the range A1:B4. If the user had entered **3** then cell F6 would say **Blue**.

The formula used to do this is shown below.

1	=LOOKUP(E6,A1:B4)		

3.3 Paste special

Sometimes you may wish to copy certain aspects of a cell or a range of cells to a different location, but you do not wish to copy all aspects of the original cell or range.

For example, in the spreadsheet on the bottom of the previous page you may wish to copy the result of the formula held in cell D1 '21A64' to another cell. To copy and paste the value rather than the formulae, copy the relevant cell or cells in the normal way, then highlight another cell (say, E1 in the above example) and **right click**. From the menu that appears, choose **Paste Special. A** dialogue box will appear showing the Paste Special options.

If you choose **Values,** '21A64' would be pasted into cell E1 rather than the formula from D1. Experiment with the other paste special options yourself.

3.4 Net Present Value (NPV) and Internal Rate of Return (IRR)

The NPV and IRR functions are best explained through a worked example. Suppose an organisation is considering undertaking a project, the financial details of which are shown below.

Project: new network system for administration department

Development and hardware purchase costs (all incurred now)		£150,000
Operating costs of new system (cash outflows per annum)	£55,000	
Annual savings from new system (cash inflow)	£115,000	
Annual net savings (net cash inflows)		£60,000
Expected system life	4 years	
Required return on investment	15% pa	

An **NPV calculation** for this project could be performed in Excel as follows.

	A	B	C
1	**NPV calculation**		
2			£
3	Costs incurred now		(150,000)
4	Benefits in year 1	60,000	
5	Benefits in year 2	60,000	
6	Benefits in year 3	60,000	
7	Benefits in year 4	60,000	
8	Discounted value		171,299
9	**Net present value**		21,299
10			
11	**Variables**		
12			
13	Discount rate	15%	

The underlying formula are shown below, together with the 'function wizard' entries used (click on the *fx* symbol in the toolbar, or select Insert, Function, to start the function wizard – NPV and IRR are **Financial** functions).

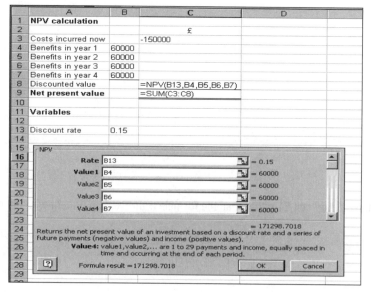

In this example, the present value of the expected **benefits** of the project **exceed** the present value of its **costs**, all discounted at 15% pa, and so the project is financially **justifiable** because it would be expected to earn a yield greater than the minimum target return of 15%. Payback of the development costs and hardware costs of £150,000 would occur after 2½ years.

An internal rate of return (**IRR**) calculation requires you to calculate the **rate of return** on a project or investment and then **compare** this rate of return with the **cost of capital**.

If a project earns a higher rate of return than the cost of capital, it will have a positive NPV and should therefore go ahead (from a financial point of view).

If the rate of return is lower than the cost of capital, the NPV will be negative - the project is not financially worthwhile.

If a project earns a return which is exactly equal to the cost of capital, the NPV will be 0, meaning the project will break-even financially.

In our example the IRR is 22%, easily exceeding the cost of capital of 15%. The IRR calculation may be set up using the function wizard (click on the **fx** symbol in the toolbar, or select **Insert**, **Function**, to start the function wizard – NPV and IRR are **Financial** functions).

	A	B	C	D
1	**IRR calculation**			
2		£		
3	Costs incurred now	-150000		
4	Benefits in year 1	60000		
5	Benefits in year 2	60000		
6	Benefits in year 3	60000		
7	Benefits in year 4	60000		
8				
9	IRR	=IRR(B3:B7)		
10				
11				

IRR

Values	B3:B7 = {-150000;60000;60(
Guess	15 = 15

= 0.218622696

Returns the internal rate of return for a series of cash flows.

    Guess is a number that you guess is close to the result of IRR; 0.1 (10 percent) if omitted.

Formula result =0.218622696   [OK]   [Cancel]

	A	B
1	**IRR calculation**	
2		£
3	Costs incurred now	(150,000)
4	Benefits in year 1	60,000
5	Benefits in year 2	60,000
6	Benefits in year 3	60,000
7	Benefits in year 4	60,000
8		
9	IRR	22%
10		

4 Database functions within Excel

Spreadsheet packages are **not true databases**, but they often have database-like facilities for manipulating tables of data, if only to a limited extent compared with a true database.

4.1 Sorting

Data in a range of cells may be sorted using Excel's Sort facility. The Sort function allows users to sort column and row data in ascending or descending order. This allows the user to customise how data is displayed. To sort data held within an Excel spreadsheet follow the steps below.

Step 1. Open the spreadsheet and highlight the range of cells containing the data you wish to Sort.

Step 2. To sort the data selected, chose **Data, Sort** from the main menu. The Sort dialogue box appears.

Step 3. In the Sort dialogue box, specify the column the data should be sorted on and the order (ascending or descending). Click OK. The data will be sorted according to your specification.

Note. To quickly sort data in ascending order, click on the button. To **Undo** a Sort go to **Edit, Undo** immediately following the sort.

4.2 Example: spreadsheets and databases

The following table contains data relating to stock and stock control.

	A	B	C	D	E	F	G	H	I
1	Component	Product	Quantity	In stock	Re-order level	Free stock	Reorder quantity	On order	Supplier
2	A001	A	1	371	160	211	400	-	P750
3	A002	B	5	33	40	-	100	100	P036
4	A003	A	5	206	60	146	150	-	P888
5	A004	D	3	176	90	86	225	-	P036
6	A005	E	9	172	120	52	300	-	P750
7	A006	C	7	328	150	178	375	-	P684
8	A007	C	2	13	10	3	25	-	P227
9	A008	C	6	253	60	193	150	-	P036
10	A009	E	9	284	90	194	225	-	P888
11	A010	B	3	435	100	335	250	-	P720
12	A011	B	2	295	110	185	275	-	P036
13	A012	A	3	40	190	-	475	475	P036
14	A013	A	7	23	120	-	300	300	P227
15	A014	C	4	296	110	186	275	-	P750
16	A015	D	7	432	40	392	100	-	P684
17	A016	D	4	416	100	316	250	-	P141
18	A017	A	3	463	150	313	375	-	P888

If you scrutinise the table you may notice that there are certain common items. For instance both components A001 and A003 are used to make Product A. Both components A001 and A005 are bought from supplier P750.

Excel allows us to **manipulate** this data, for example to see a full list of all components used to make product A, or a list of all components supplied by supplier P750. We would do this using the options available under the Data menu.

The illustration below shows what would happen if, from the **Data** menu, the user chose the option **Filter … Auto filter.** A downward pointing arrow appears beside each heading. Clicking on an arrow next to a heading results in a list of options displaying.

	A	B	C	D	E	F	G	H	I	
1	Component ▼	Product ▼	Quantity ▼	In stock ▼	Re-order level ▼	Free stock ▼	Reorder quantity ▼	On order ▼	Supplier ▼	
2	A001	A	1	371	160	211	400	-	(All)	
3	A002	B	5	33	40	-	100	100	(Top 10…) (Custom…)	
4	A003	A	5	206	60	146	150	-	P036	
5	A004	D	3	176	90	86	225	-	P141 P227	
6	A005	E	9	172	120	52	300	-	P684	
7	A006	C	7	328	150	178	375	-	P720	
8	A007	C	2	13	10	3	25	-	P750 P888	
9	A008	C	6	253	60	193	150	-	P036	
10	A009	E	9	284	90	194	225	-	P888	
11	A010	B	3	435	100	335	250	-	P720	
12	A011	B	2	295	110	185	275	-	P036	
13	A012	A	3	40	190	-	475	475	P036	
14	A013	A	7	23	120	-	300	300	P227	
15	A014	C	4	296	110	186	275	-	P750	
16	A015	D	7	432	40	392	100	-	P684	
17	A016	D	4	416	100	316	250	-	P141	
18	A017	A	3	463	150	313	375	-	P888	

Sheet1 / Sheet2 / Sheet3 /

In this illustration the user has clicked on the arrow in the Supplier column and is about to select Supplier P750. When supplier P750 is selected, the spreadsheet filters the data as shown below.

	A	B	C	D	E	F	G	H	I	
1	Component ▼	Product ▼	Quantity ▼	In stock ▼	Re-order level ▼	Free stock ▼	Reorder quantity ▼	On order ▼	Supplier ▼	
2	A001	A	1	371	160	211	400	-	P750	
6	A005	E	9	172	120	52	300	-	P750	
15	A014	C	4	296	110	186	275	-	P750	

Sheet1 / Sheet2 / Sheet3 /

The result tells us that supplier P750 supplies components A001, A005 and A014, that there is nothing on order from this supplier at present, that this supplier is important for products A, E and C only, and so on.

The original display could be reinstated by clicking on the Supplier arrow and choosing All. We could then, for example, click on the arrow in the **Product** column and select Product A to see at a glance all the components used for product A and all the suppliers for those components, whether any components were on order at present (possibly meaning delays in the availability of the next batch of Product A) and so on.

5 Spreadsheets and data tables

The term **data table** is used by some spreadsheet packages (for example Excel) to refer to a group of cells that show the results of changing the value of variables. Data tables can be explained using a simple example.

5.1 Example: a one-input data table

Suppose a company estimates production costs for an upcoming year at £5m **excluding** any allowance for inflation. Suppose also, that economic forecasters vary in their estimates of inflation in the coming year – estimates range from 2% to 10%.

If this were part of a **scenario** that the company was trying to model on a spreadsheet a 'data table' could be produced showing the range of effects of possible levels of inflation simply by:

- Entering the basic data.
- Entering one formula per item affected (eg production costs and profits in the example illustrated).
- Using Excel's data table tool.

Here is the problem set up on Microsoft Excel.

	A	B	C	D	E	F	G	H	I	J
1										
2	Input variable (eg inflation rate)						5%			
3	Constant (eg production costs)						£ 5,000,000			
4	Constant (eg profit before inflation is taken into consideration)						£ 475,000			
5										
6										
7				Production						
8				costs	Profit					
9				5,250,000	225,000					
10			2%							
11			3%							
12			4%							
13			5%							
14			6%							
15			7%							
16			8%							
17			9%							
18			10%							

This cell contains the formula G3 + (G3*G2) ie the production costs plus the increase due to inflation. It must be at the head of the 'answer' column for a one-input table.

This cell contains the formula G4 - (G3*G2) ie the profit (G4) less the increase in production costs due to inflation. It is positioned at the top of the answer column in a one-input table.

The cells shown here with a heavy border are selected and then the Data 'Table' menu is called up. This asks you to enter the 'column input cell' (we are varying a *column* of percentages), which is the cell with our original value of 5%, cell G2.

The following spreadsheet shows what happens after a single cell reference (G2) is entered, as prompted by the **data table menu** (read the explanation provided in the boxes on the previous spreadsheet).

	A	B	C	D	E	F	G	H	I
1									
2	Input variable (eg inflation rate)						5%		
3	Constant (eg production costs)						£5,000,000		
4	Constant (eg profit before inflation is taken into consideration)						£ 475,000		
5									
6									
7				Production					
8				costs	Profit				
9				5,250,000	225,000				
10			2%	5,100,000	375,000		The shaded cells are		
11			3%	5,150,000	325,000		automatically filled by the		
12			4%	5,200,000	275,000	◄—	spreadsheet package to show		
13			5%	5,250,000	225,000		the impact of inflation on		
14			6%	5,300,000	175,000		production costs and profits.		
15			7%	5,350,000	125,000				
16			8%	5,400,000	75,000				
17			9%	5,450,000	25,000				
18			10%	5,500,000	(25,000)				
19									
20									

5.2 Two-input data tables

It is also possible to use the data table facility if **two** of the numbers in the calculation are to be changed.

5.2.1 Example: two-input data table

Suppose the company from the previous our example is not sure that its production costs will be £5m - they could be only £4.5m or else they could be up to £5.5m. This situation could be set up in Excel as shown below.

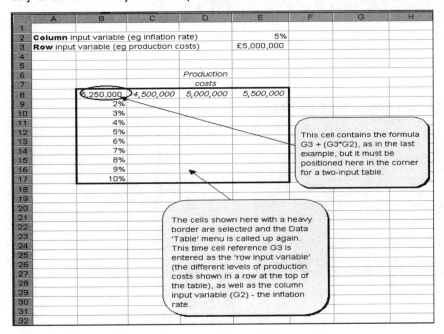

The resulting table is shown below.

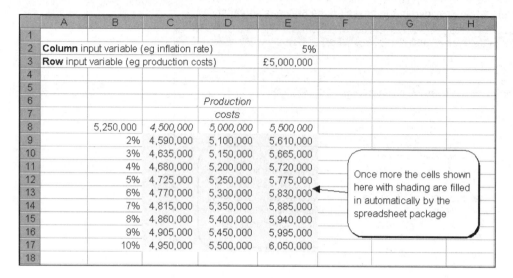

	A	B	C	D	E	F	G	H
1								
2	**Column** input variable (eg inflation rate)				5%			
3	**Row** input variable (eg production costs)				£5,000,000			
4								
5								
6				Production				
7				costs				
8		5,250,000	4,500,000	5,000,000	5,500,000			
9		2%	4,590,000	5,100,000	5,610,000			
10		3%	4,635,000	5,150,000	5,665,000			
11		4%	4,680,000	5,200,000	5,720,000			
12		5%	4,725,000	5,250,000	5,775,000			
13		6%	4,770,000	5,300,000	5,830,000			
14		7%	4,815,000	5,350,000	5,885,000			
15		8%	4,860,000	5,400,000	5,940,000			
16		9%	4,905,000	5,450,000	5,995,000			
17		10%	4,950,000	5,500,000	6,050,000			
18								

Once more the cells shown here with shading are filled in automatically by the spreadsheet package

6 Pivot tables

Excel has a powerful Pivot Table function that enables information held in tables to be extracted and manipulated quickly and easily. To create a Pivot Table, input your data into a range of cells - to form a table. To turn this into a Pivot Table, highlight the cells containing data, then select **Data** from the main menu and chose the then **Pivot Table Report** option.

This starts the Pivot Table Wizard. You are first asked to confirm the location of the data you want to analyse, then you will be presented with the following dialogue box.

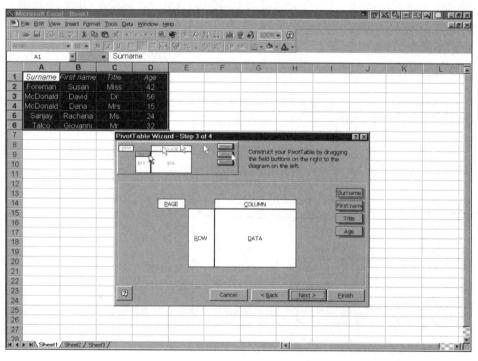

PROFESSIONAL EDUCATION

You construct your table by dragging and dropping the labelled buttons on the right into the appropriate part of the white area. For instance, if we wanted to know the total number of surnames of each type we could drag the Surname label into the row area and then drag another instance of the surname label into the Data area.

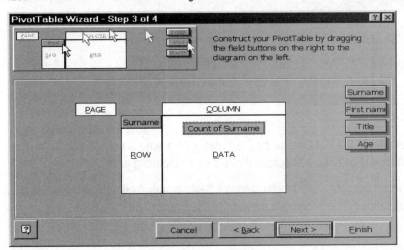

Note that in the Data area the name of the Surname label changes to Count of Surname but we do not have to accept this if it is not what we want. If we double-click on Count of Surname we are offered other options such as Sum, Average, Max, Min. For now we will accept the Count option. Clicking on Next and Finish gives the following results.

	A	B
1	Count of Surname	
2	Surname	Total
3	Foreman	1
4	McDonald	2
5	Sanjay	1
6	Talco	1
7	Grand Total	5

More elaborate analyses than this can be produced. For instance, you could try setting up a pivot table like the one below.

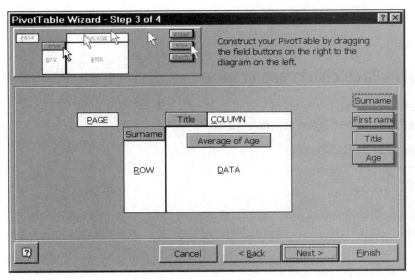

The result is as follows, showing that the average age of people called McDonald is 35.5 and the average age overall is 33.8.

	A	B	C	D	E	F	G
1	Average of Age	Title					
2	Surname	Dr	Miss	Mr	Mrs	Ms	Grand Total
3	Foreman		42				42
4	McDonald	56			15		35.5
5	Sanjay					24	24
6	Talco			32			32
7	Grand Total	56	42	32	15	24	33.8

This arrangement of the data also draws attention to the fact that the data includes a 'Mrs' who is only 15 years old. This is not impossible, but it is quite unusual and should be checked because it could be an inputting error.

If we don't happen to like the way Excel arranges the data it can be changed in a flash, simply by dragging the labels in the results to another part of the table. For instance if Title is dragged down until it is over cell B3 the data is automatically rearranged as follows.

	A	B	C
1	Average of Age		
2	Surname	Title	Total
3	Foreman	Miss	42
4	Foreman Total		42
5	McDonald	Dr	56
6		Mrs	15
7	McDonald Total		35.5
8	Sanjay	Ms	24
9	Sanjay Total		24
10	Talco	Mr	32
11	Talco Total		32
12	Grand Total		33.8

Pivot tables really come into their own when the user wishes to analyse a large amount of numeric data in a number of ways.

7 Charts and graphs

7.1 Using Microsoft Excel to produce charts and graphs

Using Microsoft Excel, it is possible to display data held in a range of spreadsheet cells in a variety of charts or graphs. We will use the Discount Traders Ltd spreadsheet shown below to generate a chart.

	A	B	C	D	E
1	**Discount Traders Ltd**				
2	*Sales analysis - April 200X*				
3	Customer	Sales	5% discount	Sales (net)	
4		£	£	£	
5	Arthur	956.00	0.00	956.00	
6	Dent	1423.00	71.15	1351.85	
7	Ford	2894.00	144.70	2749.30	
8	Prefect	842.00	0.00	842.00	
9					
10					

The data in the spreadsheet could be used to generate a chart, such as those shown below. We explain how later in this section.

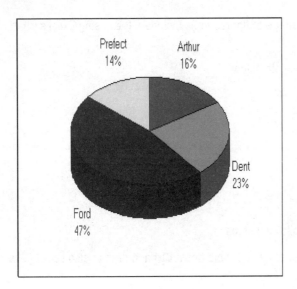

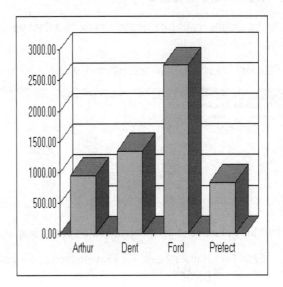

The Chart Wizard, which we explain in a moment, may also be used to generate a line graph. A line graph would normally be used to track a trend over time. For example, the chart below graphs the Total Revenue figures shown in Row 7 of the following spreadsheet.

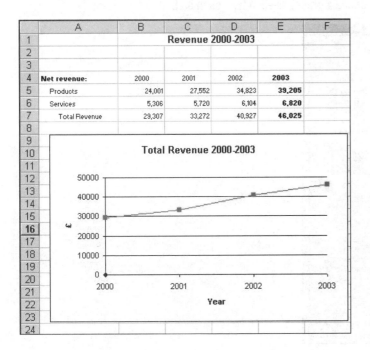

7.2 The Chart Wizard

Charts and graphs may be generated simply by **selecting the range** of figures to be included, then using Excel's Chart Wizard.

The Discount Traders spreadsheet referred to earlier is shown again below.

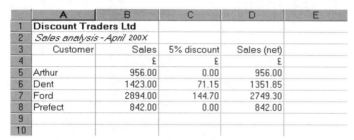

	A	B	C	D	E
1	**Discount Traders Ltd**				
2	*Sales analysis – April 200X*				
3	Customer	Sales	5% discount	Sales (net)	
4		£	£	£	
5	Arthur	956.00	0.00	956.00	
6	Dent	1423.00	71.15	1351.85	
7	Ford	2894.00	144.70	2749.30	
8	Prefect	842.00	0.00	842.00	
9					
10					

To chart the **net sales** of the different **customers**, follow the following steps.

Step 1. Highlight cells A5:A8, then move your pointer to cell D5, hold down **Ctrl** and drag to also select cells D5:D8.

Step 2. Look at the **toolbar** at the top of your spreadsheet. You should see an **icon** that looks like a small bar chart. Click on this icon to start the 'Chart Wizard'.

The following steps are taken from the Excel 2000 Chart Wizard. Other versions may differ slightly.

Step 3. Pick the type of chart you want. We will choose chart type **Column** and then select the sub-type we think will be most effective. (To produce a graph, select a type such as **Line**).

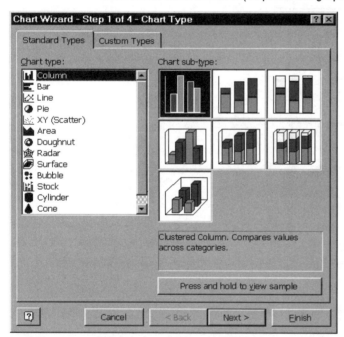

PROFESSIONAL EDUCATION

Step 4. This step gives us the opportunity to confirm that the data we selected earlier was correct and to decide whether the chart should be based on **columns** (eg Customer, Sales, Discount etc) or **rows** (Arthur, Dent etc). We can accept the default values and click Next.

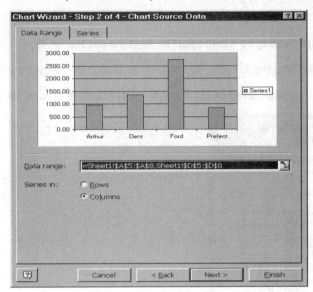

Step 5. Next, specify your chart **title** and axis **labels**. Incidentally, one way of remembering which is the **X axis** and which is the **Y axis** is to look at the letter Y: it is the only letter that has a vertical part pointing straight up, so it must be the vertical axis! Click Next to move on.

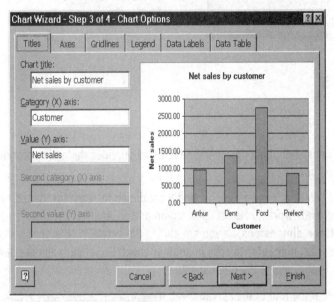

As you can see, there are other index tabs available. You can see the effect of selecting or deselecting each one in **preview** - experiment with these options as you like then click Next.

Step 6. The final step is to choose whether you want the chart to appear on the same worksheet as the data or on a separate sheet of its own. This is a matter of personal preference – for this example choose to place the chart as an object within the existing spreadsheet.

7.3 Changing existing charts

Even after your chart is 'finished', you can change it.

    (a)   You can **resize it** simply by selecting it and dragging out its borders.

    (b)   You can change **each element** by **double clicking** on it then selecting from the options available.

    (c)   You could also select any item of **text** and alter the wording, size or font, or change the **colours** used.

    (d)   In the following illustration, the user has double-clicked on the Y axis to enable them to **change the scale**.

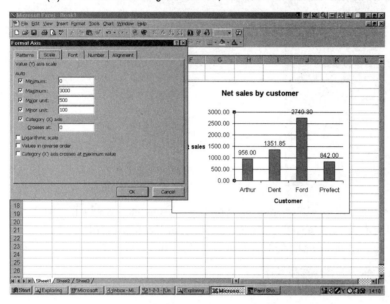

8 Multi-sheet spreadsheets

8.1 Background

In early spreadsheet packages, a spreadsheet file consisted of a single worksheet. Excel provides the option of multi-sheet spreadsheets, consisting of a series of related sheets.

For example, suppose you were producing a profit forecast for two regions, and a combined forecast for the total of the regions. This situation would be suited to using separate worksheets for each region and another for the total. This approach is sometimes referred to as working in **three dimensions**, as you are able to flip between different sheets stacked in front or behind each other. Cells in one sheet may **refer** to cells in another sheet. So, in our example, the formulae in the cells in the total sheet would refer to the cells in the other sheets.

Excel has a series of 'tabs', one for each worksheet at the foot of the spreadsheet.

8.2 How many sheets?

Excel can be set up so that it always opens a fresh file with a certain number of worksheets ready and waiting for you. Click on **Tools ... Options** ... and then the **General** tab and set the number *Sheets in new workbook* option to the number you would like each new spreadsheet file to contain. (Sheets may be added or deleted later.)

PROFESSIONAL EDUCATION

If you subsequently want to insert more sheets you just **right click** on the index tab after which you want the new sheet to be inserted and choose **Insert** ... and then **Worksheet**. By default sheets are called **Sheet 1, Sheet 2** etc. However, these may be changed. To **rename** a sheet in **Excel, right click** on its index tab and choose the rename option.

8.3 Pasting from one sheet to another

When building a spreadsheet that will contain a number of worksheets with identical structure, users often set up one sheet, then copy that sheet and amend the sheet contents. [To copy a worksheet in Excel, from within the worksheet you wish to copy, select Edit, Move or Copy sheet, and tick the Create a copy box.] A 'Total' sheet would use the same structure, but would contain formulae totalling the individual sheets.

8.4 Linking sheets with formulae

Formulae on one sheet may refer to data held on another sheet. The links within such a formula may be established using the following steps.

Step 1. In the cell that you want to refer to a cell from another sheet, type =.

Step 2. Click on the index tab for the sheet containing the cell you want to refer to and select the cell in question.

Step 3. Press Enter or Return.

We'll look at a very simple example. Start with a blank spreadsheet and ensure that it contains at least two sheets.

Type the number 1,746, 243 in cell A1 of the first sheet. Then select the tab for the second sheet and select A1 in that sheet (this is step 1 from the three steps above). Type =. Follow steps 2 and 3 above. The same number will display in cell A1 of both sheets. However, what is actually contained in cell A1 of the second sheet is the formula =**Sheet1!A1**

Cell A1 in the second sheet is now linked to cell A1 in the first sheet. This method may be used regardless of the cell addresses - the two cells **do not have to be in the same place** in their respective sheets. For instance cell Z658 of one sheet could refer to cell P24 of another. If you **move cells** or insert **extra rows** or columns on the sheet with the original numbers the cell references on the other sheet will **change automatically**.

8.5 Uses for multi-sheet spreadsheets

There are a wide range of situations suited to the multi-sheet approach. A variety of possible uses follow.

(a) A model could use one sheet for variables, a second for calculations, and a third for outputs.

(b) To enable quick and easy **consolidation** of similar sets of data, for example the financial results of two subsidiaries or the budgets of two departments.

(c) To provide **different views** of the same data. For instance you could have one sheet of data sorted in product code order and another sorted in product name order.

9 Macros

A macro is a sort of mini-program that automates keystrokes or actions. Macros are often used within spreadsheets. Macros may be written using a type of code – like a programming language. However, most spreadsheet users produce macros by asking the spreadsheet to record their actions – this automatically generates the macro 'code' required.

Macros can get **very complex** indeed – in fact you **can** build whole applications using them. (Doing so is a very good introduction to programming proper.)

We are **not** going to be demonstrating anything very elaborate, here. We are just going to show you how macros can be used to **eliminate a few key-strokes and mouse clicks** for tasks that you have to **perform frequently** enough to warrant writing a macro in the first place.

We are going to explain the basic principles of macros by reference to Microsoft **Excel**.

9.1 A simple macro

Suppose you decided that **every spreadsheet you created** should have your **first name and surname** in the bottom right corner of the footer in **Arial 8pt font**. You could write a macro and do all of this just by pressing two keys.

To write this macro you would proceed as follows. Follow this example through **hands-on** if possible.

> **Step 1.** **Excel:** Open a fresh file. Click on the **Tools** menu and then on the option **Macro**
>
> **Step 2.** This gives a sub-menu including the option **Record New Macro**. Select this.
>
> **Step 3.** A dialogue box like the following will appear.

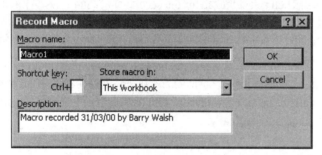

> **Step 4.** Give the macro a name such as InsertName and press **Tab**. Excel will not allow spaces within macro names.
>
> **Step 5.** Choose a shortcut key. This must be a **letter**, and it should be one that you don't frequently use for other purposes such as Ctrl + C or Ctrl + B. We will choose **Ctrl + m**
>
> (Note that we use lower case **m;** if we had used **M** we would subsequently have to type Ctrl +**Shift** +m to start the macro).
>
> **Step 6.** Accept the option to store the macro in **This Workbook** and **click on OK**
>
> **Step 7.** Everything you do is now being **recorded**.
>
> **Step 8.** From the menu select **View, Header and Footer.**

Step 9. Click on **Custom Footer** and click into the **Right section**.

Step 10. Type your name and highlight the text by clicking and dragging the cursor over it.

Step 11. Click on the **A** button to activate the font menu, and select Arial 8pt.

Step 12. Close the menus by clicking on **OK**. (Three **OK** boxes require clicking.)

Step 13. Click on the stop recording button.

Always start a macro by **returning the cursor to cell A1** (by pressing Ctrl + Home), even if it is already there. You may well not want to make your first entry in cell A1, but if you select your first real cell (B4 say) **before** you start recording, the macro will always begin at the currently active cell, whether it is B4 or Z256.

Always finish a macro by **selecting the cell** where the **next entry** is required.

That's all there is to it. Test your macro now by **selecting a fresh sheet** and then pressing Ctrl + m together. Then type 'Test' in cell A1 (as Excel will not Print Preview a blank sheet), and select **File, Print Preview.** You will see your name has been inserted into the footer.

Save your file with a suitable name and **close down** your spreadsheet package completely. Then open it up again and open a completely **new file**. Press Ctrl + m. Regrettably, nothing will happen. This does not mean that your macro is lost forever, just that it is not currently in the computer's memory (because you closed down the package).

However, if you **open up the file you just saved**, your macro will work again, because it is actually **stored** in that file. If you want your macro to be **available to you whenever** you want it you have the following choices.

(a) Keep this file, with no contents other than your 'name' macro (and any others you may write) and always use it as the basis for any new spreadsheets you create, which will subsequently be saved with new file names.

(b) You can add the macro to your **Personal Macro Workbook.** You do this at the point when you are naming your workbook and choosing a shortcut key, by changing the option in the **Store macro in:** box from This Workbook to Personal Macro Workbook. The macro will then be loaded into memory whenever you start up Excel and be available in any spreadsheet you create.

If you forget to assign a keyboard shortcut to a macro (or do not want to do so), you can still run your macros by clicking on Tools …Macro … Macros. This gives you a list of all the macros currently available. Select the one you want then click on Run.

Do not accept the default names offered by Excel of Macro1, Macro2 etc. You will soon forget what these macros do, unless you give them a meaningful name.

Key learning points

☑   A **spreadsheet** is basically an electronic piece of paper divided into **rows** and **columns**. The intersection of a row and a column is known as a **cell**.

☑   **Relative** cell references (B3) change when you copy formulae to other locations or move data from one place to another. **Absolute** cell references ($B$3) stay the same.

☑   Spreadsheets also offer **database** facilities for **manipulating** and **sorting** tables of data. **Filters** can be applied at the click of a button and these allow the user to view a large spreadsheet with only selected items of data showing.

☑   A **data table** is a special facility that can be set up so that a group of cells show the results of changing the value of variables.

☑   A **pivot table** is an interactive table that summarises and analyses data from existing lists and tables.

☑   **Functions** such as LEFT and LOOKUP and **operators** such as & can be helpful when manipulating data in a spreadsheet. **Financial** functions such as **NPV** and **IRR** may be used to simplify complex financial calculations.

☑   Excel's **Chart Wizard** makes the process of charting or graphing data held in a spreadsheet relatively simple.

☑   A **macro** is an automated process that may be written by recording key-strokes and mouse clicks. This is useful for automating frequently repeated tasks.

☑   Spreadsheets can be used in a variety of accounting contexts. You should practise using spreadsheets, **hands-on experience** is the key to spreadsheet proficiency.

Quick quiz

1   Which function key may be used to change cell references within a selected formula from absolute to relative – and vice-versa?

2   You are about to key an exam mark into cell B4 of a spreadsheet. Write an IF statement, to be placed in cell C4, that will display PASS in C4 if the student mark is 50 or above - and or will display FAIL if the mark is below 50 (all student marks are whole numbers).

3   Give two ways of starting Excel's function wizard.

4   What feature of Excel would you use to copy the formats (and only the formats) of a cell or range of cells from one area of a spreadsheet to another area?

5   Under which item from the Excel main menu is the Pivot Table Report option?

6   What formula would be used in worksheet *Sheet2* to refer to cell D5 in worksheet *Sheet1*?

Answers to quick quiz

1   The F4 key.

2   =IF(A4>49,"PASS","FAIL ")

3   You could click on the *fx* symbol in the toolbar, or use the menu item Insert, Function, to start the function wizard.

4   The Pate Special feature – then select Formats from within the Paste Special dialogue box.

5   Data.

6   =Sheet1!D5 (you would not need to type this, you would enter = in the cell you wish the value to display, then navigate using the mouse to cell D5 in worksheet Sheet1 and hit Enter).

P A R T   B

Practice activities

Activity 1

Open the spreadsheet **Ac_01_Q**. If you have installed the files provided on the CD-ROM that came with this book, you will find the file in the folder **C:\BPPTECH** on your hard drive.

If you have not installed these files yet, do so now. See pages (v) and (vi).

You will see a spreadsheet like the following.

	A	B	C	D	E	F
1						
2						
3			**Name**	Paula		
4			**Age**	24		
5						
6						
7						
8						
9						
10			**Name**	**Age**		
11			Annette	38		
12			Josephine	43		
13			Mike	32		
14			Paula	24		
15						

Replace the current contents of cell D3 (Paula) by entering one of the other names shown in cells C11 to C13. Explain what happens to the Age displayed in cell D4.

Activity 2

Open the spreadsheet **Ac_02_Q** from the folder BPPTECH. The sheet will look like illustration below.

The spreadsheet the chargeout rates of accountants of different grades in an audit firm, and the hours over a two week period they spent working on the audit of a particular client.

The accountants are identified by a four character personnel number such as Q001.

	A	B	C	D	E	F	G	H
1	Grade	Chargeout Rate (£/hour)			Employee	Grade	Hours	
2	1	20.00			Q021	3	7	
3	2	17.50			P004	1	20	
4	3	16.00			P004	1	5	
5	4	14.25			P004	1	29	
6	5	12.50			P007	3	9	
7					U003	4	7	
8					D022	3	30	
9					D022	3	15	
10					P007	3	15	
11					P012	2	19	
12					Q001	5	19	
13					F001	5	3	
14					C015	4	14	
15					C015	4	28	
16					Q005	3	17	
17					F001	5	2	
18					Q001	5	16	
19					U011	2	30	
20					A047	3	1	
21					A047	3	34	
22					Q021	3	7	
23					U002	2	20	
24					U011	2	15	
25					Q021	3	13	
26					P004	1	8	
27					Q021	3	19	
28					P012	2	9	
29					U003	4	17	
30					Q005	3	29	
31					U002	2	26	
32								

Using the LOOKUP skill you learned in Activity 1, calculate the total to bill this client for the audit work done.

Activity 3

You work for a business called Dunraven, which uses a manual accounting system. You are faced with the task of producing the trial balance at the end of the year to 30 June 20X6. The following balances have been extracted from the ledgers.

	£
Revenue	336,247
Purchases	224,362
Carriage	6,184
Drawings	14,686
Rent and rates	14,621
Postage and stationery	5,789
Advertising	2,941
Salaries and wages	56,934
Bad debt expense	1,614
Provision for bad debts	365
Debtors	31,050
Creditors	9,456
Cash in hand	422
Cash at bank	2,136
Inventory as at 1 July 20X5	15,605
Equipment: at cost	116,000
accumulated depreciation	55,400
Equity	90,876

The following additional information comes to light.

(a)   Of the carriage costs, £1,624 represents carriage inwards on purchases.

(b)   Rates are payable 6 months in advance. A payment of £2,120 made on 30 June 20X6 represents rates for July to December 20X7.

(c)   A rent demand for £510 for the three months ended 30 June 20X6 was not received until 1 July 20X6.

(d)   Equipment is to be depreciated at 15% per annum using the straight line method.

(e)   The provision for bad debts is to be increased to 2% of debtors.

(f)   Closing inventory was £31,529.

Task

Prepare an extended trial balance using a spreadsheet package.

Activity 4

At the last minute, you are instructed to change the depreciation rate for equipment to 20% per annum straight line method.

Task

Update your spreadsheet in Activity 3 to reflect this change of policy, which will not affect prior years.

Activity 5

The following balances were extracted from the ledger accounts of Oaklands, a trader, at 31 December 20X4. These figures are available already entered for you in the file **Ac_05_Q** in your BPP data.

	£
Freehold land and buildings	25,000
Furniture & fittings: cost	3,360
: accumulated depreciation	2,016
Motor cars: cost	1,900
: accumulated depreciation	980
Debtors	16,121
Creditors	9,125
Bank	4,873
Provision for doubtful debts at 1.1.20X4	792
Inventory at 1.1.20X4	10,858
Revenue	142,125
Purchases	101,286
Rent received	810
Car expenses	841
Bad debt expense	943
General expenses	1,842
Rent and rates	2,414
Wages and salaries	18,103
Discounts allowed	3,125
Equity	44,550
Drawings	9,732

PROFESSIONAL EDUCATION

You also have the following information.

(a)   Inventory at 31 December 20X4 was £12,654.

(b)   Rates paid in advance at 31 December 20X4 were £106.

(c)   It has been decided to reduce the provision for doubtful debts to 4% of debtors as at 31 December 20X4.

(d)   The tenant owes £268 in rent at 31 December 20X4.

(e)   Wages and salaries accrued at 31 December 20X4 were £421.

(f)   Depreciation is to be provided as for 20X3.

(g)   Unused stamps in the franking machine as at 31 December 20X4 amounted to £86.

Task

Using the file **Ac_05_Q,** or a copy of its data, prepare an extended trial balance as at 31 December 20X4.

Activity 6

When you have completed the spreadsheet in Activity 5, there is a change of depreciation policy for the motor car. It is now proposed to provide depreciation at 25% on the reducing balance.

Task

Amend your spreadsheet accordingly.

Activity 7

In the spreadsheet below, only the cells A1 and A2 contain data. Cells B1:D2 contain formulae.

	A	B	C	D
1	23/02/2001	23	2	2001
2	31/12/2001	31	12	2001
3	311			

Task

What do you think the formulae are? (Use Excel's Help facility if necessary.) What is the result of subtracting cell A1 from cell A2?

Activity 8

Goodwood, a furniture-making business manufactures quality furniture to customers' orders. It has three production departments and two service departments. Budgeted overhead costs for the coming year, 20X6, are as follows.

	Total £
Rent and rates	12,800
Machine insurance	6,000
Telephone charges	3,200
Depreciation	18,000
Production supervisor	24,000
Heat and light	6,400
	70,400

The three production departments - A, B and C and the two service departments X and Y are housed in the new premises, the details of which, together with other statistics and information are given below.

	Departments				
	A	B	C	X	Y
Floor area occupied (sq metres)	3,000	1,800	600	600	400
Machine value (£'000s)	24	10	8	4	2
Direct labour hrs budgeted	3,200	1,800	1,000		
Labour rates per hour	£3.80	£3.50	£3.40	£3.00	£3.00
Allocated overheads					
Specific to each department (£'000s)	2.8	1.7	1.2	0.8	0.6
Service department X's costs apportioned	50%	25%	25%		
Service department Y's costs apportioned	20%	30%	50%		

Tasks

(a)   Prepare a spreadsheet showing the overhead cost budgeted for each department. Use the following bases of apportionment.

Overhead item	*Basis of apportionment*
Allocated costs	Specific to dept
Rent and rates	Floor area
Machine insurance	Machine value
Telephone charges	Floor area
Depreciation	Machine value
Production supervisor	Direct labour hours
Heat and light	Floor area

(b)   Calculate overhead absorption rates for each department based on direct labour hours.

Activity 9

The budgeted overheads in Activity 8 have been revised as follows.

Rent and rates	Up by 5%
Machine insurance	Up by 10%
Telephone charges	Up by 25%
Depreciation	Unchanged
Production supervision	Up by 2.8%
Heat and light	Down by 8%

Task

Amend your spreadsheet accordingly.

Activity 10

The partners at a small firm of solicitors are trying to assess their likely income from conveyancing in the next year. They charge a standard fee of £300 for conveyancing work. On average they reckon that a conveyancing job takes about 5 hours but this varies considerably from case to case due to the large number of unknown factors involved.

Years of experience enable them to assess the likely difficulty of a job (based on their knowledge of the other solicitor involved, the lending organisation, the local authority, the price of the property and so on). They have assigned weighting factors to as many of the variables as possible such that an average job has a total weighting factor of 1. They have a policy of refusing any jobs with a total weighting factor greater than 2.

The most likely scenario for the coming year has been set up on a spreadsheet as follows.

	A	B	C	D	E	F	G	H
1								
2	Standard fee £	300						
3	Number of clients	100						
4	Average time (hours)	5		Fee income formula **isn't** affected by the variability index as jobs are charged out at a flat rate =B2*B3				
5	Variable costs per hour (£)	20						
6	Fixed costs per annum (£)	5,000						
7								
8	Variability index	1.00						
9								
10		£						
11	Fee income	30,000		The variable cost formula **is** affected by the variability index: =-(B5*B4*B3)*B8				
12	Variable costs	(10,000)						
13	Fixed costs	(5,000)						
14	Net profit	15,000						
15								
16								

These figures are available already entered for you in the file **Ac_10_Q** in your BPP data.

Task

A data table is needed to assess the consequences of different scenarios. The top left hand corner and the row variable and column variables are shown below. Complete the spreadsheet to calculate the figures that will appear in the data table.

	A	B	C	D	E	F	G	H
18	=B14	0.50	0.75	1.00	1.25	1.50	1.75	2.00
19	0							
20	25							
21	50							
22	75							
23	100							
24	125							
25	150							
26	200							
27	225							
28	250							

What will be the net profit if 125 jobs are taken on with an overall average weighting factor of 1.25?

Activity 11

You work in the accounts department of International Magazines Limited (IML). IML publish four magazines, which are sold throughout the world. One of the spreadsheets you work on analyses sales by magazine and world region.

This spreadsheet is shown below, and is available as the file **Ac_11_Q** in the BPP data files. Open this file now.

	A	B	C	D	E	F
1	International Magazines Limited: Sales by Region Jan-Jun 2003					
2		Europe	America	Rest of the world	Total	
3	Woman's Day	251,208	163,514	105,000 £	519,722	
4	Blue!	202,262	136,290	78,485 £	417,036	
5	Easy Cooking	143,588	86,040	114,900 £	344,528	
6	Sorted!	27,795	6,234	14,769 £	48,798	
7	Total	£ 624,852	£ 392,078	£ 313,154	£ 1,330,083	
8						

Tasks

(a) Follow the instructions below to create a column chart using the Chart Wizard.

   (i) Select cells **A2:D6** (ensure these are the only cells selected, do not include the totals).

   (ii) Click the Chart Wizard button on the standard toolbar (shown below). *If the Office Assistant pops up at this, or at any other time, click 'No, don't provide help now' to close it.*

   (iii) Accept the default **Column** chart type and the Clustered Column chart sub-type by clicking **Next**.

   (iv) Accept the **Columns** option by clicking **Next**.

   (v) If necessary click the **Titles** tab, click the **Chart title** box and type 'Sales by magazine and region Jan-Jun 2003'. Click **Next**.

(vi)   Accept the default option to create the chart as an object within the Sales Data sheet by clicking on **Finish**.

(vii) Click anywhere outside the chart to deselect it, then save the file.

(b)   Follow the instructions below to change the size and position of the chart.

(i)   Click anywhere inside the white area of the chart border to select it. Square 'handles' appear on the chart border.

(ii)   Position the pointer inside the chart near the border (well away from the Title). Click and hold down the mouse button and start to drag the chart down and to the left. The pointer changes to a four pointer 'compass' as you drag. Position the top left corner of the chart in cell A13 and release the mouse button.

(iii) With the chart still selected, position the pointer on the bottom right selection handle. When the pointer changes to a diagonal two headed arrow, hold down the mouse button and drag the selection handle downward to the right until the chart reaches the right edge of column F and row 35. Release the mouse button.

(iv)   Click anywhere outside the chart to deselect it, then save the file.

(c)   Follow the instructions below to add a title to the Y axis.

(i)   Click anywhere inside the white area of the chart border to select it.

(ii)   From the main menu at the top of the screen click **Chart**, then **Chart Options**.

(iii) If not already selected, click the **Titles** tab. Click into the **Value (Y) axis** box and type 'Sales (£)', then click **OK**. Click anywhere outside the chart to deselect it.

(d)   Add a suitable footer to the Sales Data sheet that includes your name and ensure the sheet is set up to print the figures and graph clearly and on one page. Save the file. (Use Excel's Help facility to Search for Help on any function you are unsure of.)

You have now completed Activity 11. You may wish to check your work against the BPP answer in the file **Ac_11_S**

> After completing this Activity, you may like to perform it again choosing a different type of chart and experimenting with the fonts and styles of the title and labels.

Activity 12

Open the file **Ac_12_Q** in your BPP data. An extract from this spreadsheet is shown below.

	A	B	C	D
1	Issue No	Quantity	Colour	Shape
2	1473	159	Blue	Square
3	1474	84	Yellow	Square
4	1475	120	Green	Triangular
5	1476	125	Blue	Round
6	1477	153	Yellow	Triangular
7	1478	99	Blue	Round
8	1479	137	Blue	Triangular
9	1480	199	Red	Square
10	1481	16	Red	Round
11	1482	158	Green	Square
12	1483	29	Red	Triangular
13	1484	118	Yellow	Square
14	1485	167	Blue	Round
15	1486	177	Red	Triangular
16	1487	168	Green	Square
17	1488	110	Red	Round
18	1489	181	Red	Square
19	1490	168	Blue	Square
20	1491	31	Red	Square
21	1492	86	Green	Triangular
22	1493	160	Green	Triangular
23	1494	120	Red	Square
24	1495	101	Blue	Triangular
25	1496	141	Red	Triangular
26	1497	187	Blue	Triangular
27	1498	62	Green	Square
28	1499	177	Blue	Triangular
29	1500	148	Green	Square
30	1501	175	Red	Triangular
31	1502	131	Red	Square
32	1503	67	Blue	Square
33	1504	18	Blue	Round

The spreadsheet shows the quantity of components of various types that were issued from stores to production during a period. Components come in four colours (Blue, Red, Green and Yellow) and three shapes (Square, Round and Triangular). You will be using Microsoft Excel's Pivot Table feature to analyse and summarise this data.

Tasks

(a)   Position the cursor anywhere in columns A to D and rows 1 to 100, for instance in cell A1 or cell C24.

(b)   Click on **Data** in the menu bar at the top of the screen. Select the **Pivot Table Report** option.

(c)   The following screen will appear. Make sure that the option Microsoft Excel or data base is selected and then click on **Next**.

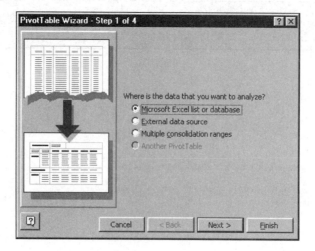

(d)   The following Window will appear. The Range you want to base your Pivot Table on is already filled in for you because you positioned your cursor within it at step (a), so you can just click on **Next>.**

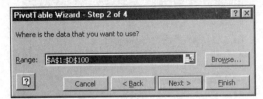

(e)   The following box will appear.

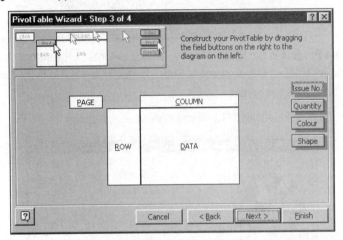

Click on the button labelled **Shape,** and keeping your left mouse button held down drag the button into the white space labelled ROW. A copy of the Shape button will be created there.

Do like wise with the button labelled **Colour** except drag it to the white space labelled COLUMN.

Do likewise with the button labelled **Quantity** but drag it into the white space labelled DATA.

The box on-screen should now look something like this.

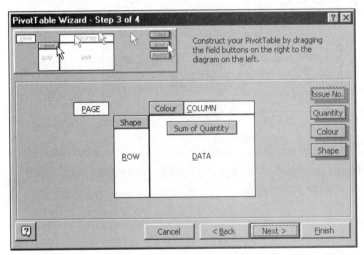

(f)   Click on the button labelled **Sum of Quantity.** A pop-up Window will appear as follows.

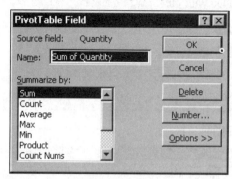

Select the word **Product** in the Summarize by: list box and watch the entry in the Name box change. In fact the option we want on this occasion is **Sum,** so select **Sum** again in the list box to make the screen look exactly like it does above. Click on **OK.**

(g)   In the main screen click on **Next>.** The following screen will appear.

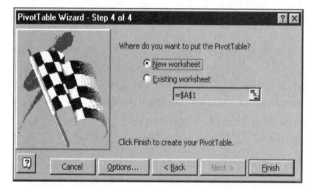

Choose the option to put the Pivot Table in a **New worksheet** and click on Finish.

The result will be as follows.

	A	B	C	D	E	F
1	Sum of Quantity	Colour				
2	Shape	Blue	Green	Red	Yellow	Grand Total
3	Round	482	584	297	824	2187
4	Square	628	1440	1240	1153	4461
5	Triangular	1195	1139	1114	782	4230
6	Grand Total	2305	3163	2651	2759	10878
7						
8						
9						

This summarises quantities of components used by shape and colour: exactly what you wanted to do, with the click of a few buttons!

(h)   Select the cell C4 (the total of square green components issued) and double click on it. The following will appear in a new sheet.

	A	B	C	D
1	Issue No.	Quantity	Colour	Shape
2	1559	68	Green	Square
3	1553	200	Green	Square
4	1550	138	Green	Square
5	1548	68	Green	Square
6	1533	63	Green	Square
7	1524	115	Green	Square
8	1519	108	Green	Square
9	1516	144	Green	Square
10	1500	148	Green	Square
11	1482	158	Green	Square
12	1498	62	Green	Square
13	1487	168	Green	Square
14				

Here you have **drilled down** to find the issue note information underlying the total of 1,440 issues of square green components.

(i)   Return to the Pivot table sheet and drag the button labelled **Colour** (in cell B1) into cell A3. The data will instantly be rearranged as follows.

	A	B	C	D
1	Sum of Quantity			
2	Colour	Shape	Total	
3	Blue	Round	482	
4		Square	628	
5		Triangular	1195	
6	Blue Total		2305	
7	Green	Round	584	
8		Square	1440	
9		Triangular	1139	
10	Green Total		3163	
11	Red	Round	297	
12		Square	1240	
13		Triangular	1114	
14	Red Total		2651	
15	Yellow	Round	824	
16		Square	1153	
17		Triangular	782	
18	Yellow Total		2759	
19	Grand Total		10878	
20				

(j)   Play with the Pivot table some more before you close it. For instance try right clicking within it and experimenting with some of the other options. (For instance the Wizard option lets you go back to the **Step 3 of 4** where you choose your layout. What is the effect of other choices of buttons and other layouts? Can you just have a button in the DATA area without specifying Row or Column? As another experiment, find out what happens to your Pivot Table if you alter the figures in the original data).

(k)   Create a copy of the original data in a fresh sheet and see if you can construct a Pivot Table on your own without looking at these instructions.

Activity 13

The accountant at Rolling Projections Ltd is preparing the cash flow forecast for the coming year. She has projected what she thinks the opening balance sheet (at 01 July 20X5) will be and wishes to prepare a 12 month (monthly) forecast.

The following information is relevant.

(a)   Projected opening Balance Sheet

	£'000	£'000
Land and buildings	220	
Plant and machinery	110	
Motor vehicles	65	
		395
Inventory	40	
Trade debtors	60	
Cash in hand	5	
	105	
Overdraft	65	
Trade creditors	35	
	100	
Net current assets		5
Long term creditors		120
Net assets		280
Share capital		100
Reserves		180
		280

(b)   Budgeted Profit and Loss Account for the year ending 30 June 20X6

	£'000
Revenue	390
Cost of sales	165
Rent and rates	60
Depreciation	30
Marketing	35
Administrative expenses	75
Selling expenses	45
Loss before interest	20

(c)   One sixth of the year's sales occur in each of the months of July and August. The rest are evenly spread over the remaining months of the year. Debtor balances are usually collected as follows.

- 10% in the month of sale
- 60% in the month following sale
- 30% in the second month after sale

The accountant expects to be able to collect 90% of opening debtor balances in July and will write off the rest.

(d)   Trade creditors are paid 20% in the month of purchase and 80% in the following month. Because she ran a large batch of cheques just before year end, the accountant does not expect to have to settle opening trade creditors until August.

The accountant is budgeting for no overall change in inventory levels. Purchases are spread evenly over the year.

(e)   Rates, which total £20,000, are paid in April, and rent (the balance on the rent and rates account) is paid in equal amounts on the Quarter Days.

(f)   The marketing budget is set at £1,000 per month excluding November. The balance will be spent on a major burst campaign in November.

(g)   Administrative expenses are spread evenly over the year.

(h)   Selling expenses are paid in the month of sale and are incurred in the same proportion as that in which sales are earned.

(i)   Interest of 2% per month is paid on any overdraft balance at the end of the month and added to the account balance. (Hint: use an IF statement.)

(j)   Cash in hand is not to be included in opening bank balances for the purpose of this projection.

Task

Prepare a monthly cash flow forecast for the year ending 30 June 20X6.

Activity 14

This Activity uses the spreadsheet created in Activity 13. The current overdraft facility for Rolling Projections Ltd stands at £50,000. Modify the original spreadsheet so that it shows in which month(s) the facility is likely to be exceeded, and by how much.

Activity 15

You have been selected to work on a special assignment at a subsidiary company. The assignment team will consist of, besides you, the divisional chief accountant, an assistant accountant and a secretary. Because you are familiar with spreadsheets, you have been asked to set up a spreadsheet to record the time which each of you spends on this assignment and to cost it using your group's internal chargeout rates, which are as follows.

	£
Divisional chief accountant	72.50
Assistant accountant	38.00
Accounting technician	21.45
Secretary	17.30

Tasks

(a) Design a spreadsheet which will show hours spent and cost per person by week for a three week assignment.

(b) Complete the spreadsheet by entering the following time data, and calculate the total personnel costs of the job.

	Week 3	Week 2	Week 1
You	37 hrs 30 mins	40 hrs	32 hrs
Assistant Accountant	35 hrs	40 hrs	20 hrs
Divisional chief accountant	6 hrs 45 mins	4 hrs 30 mins	-
Secretary	37 hrs 15 mins	32 hrs 10 mins	15 hrs

Activity 16

This Activity uses the spreadsheet created in Activity 15.

A week later, back at head office, you receive a memo from the divisional chief accountant. He tells you that he has spent a further six hours on the assignment, in week 4. He also wants you to add in to your calculations the costs of two laptop computers which were charged out at £100 per week each for the duration of the three weeks of fieldwork. You have also found out that secretarial chargeout rates were increased by 10% from week 3 onwards.

Task

Update the spreadsheet which you created in Activity 15.

Activity 17

At Bright Ideas Ltd petty cash is accounted for in an old fashioned two column cash book. You have decided to set up a cash book analysis using a spreadsheet. The following information is relevant.

(a) Petty cash receipts arise from occasional sales to customers who arrive at the factory wishing to make small purchases and who cannot be persuaded to pay by cheque or credit card.

(b) Payments out of petty cash are made for postage, stationery, kitchen supplies (such as coffee and biscuits), to purchase leaving gifts to staff and sundries such as taxi fares.

(c) At the end of each week, any excess over £250 is banked and any shortfall made up by cashing a cheque.

Task

Design a sample page for the analysed cash book, using formulae where appropriate. You should find that 20 lines are sufficient for a typical week's transactions. Receipts and payments are always to be entered on separate lines. You should ignore VAT.

Activity 18

This Activity uses the petty cash book analysis which you designed in Activity 17.

During week 37 (week ending 12 September 20X6) the following transactions take place. On the morning of Monday 8 September, there is £230 in the petty cash tin, together with an IOU for £20 signed by the Finance Director and dated the previous Friday.

Day	Ref	Transaction	Amount £
Monday	2388	Cash sale	25.60
	2389	Cash sale	13.55
	4998	Purchase of coffee	12.96
Tuesday	-	FD repayment	20.00
	2390	Cash sale	25.60
	4999	Padded envelopes	3.95
	4000	First class stamps	25.00
Wednesday	2391	Cash sale	4.00
	2392	Cash sale	13.55
	4001	Wedding present – Alison	74.99
Thursday	4002	Taxi fare	8.00
Friday	2393	Cash sale	12.00
	4003	Christian Aid collector	20.00
	4004	Speedpost packages	32.71

Task

Complete the petty cash book for the week. The final entry should show the payment to or receipt from the bank at the end of the week.

Activity 19

Bodger & Co is a jobbing company. On 1 September 20X5 there was one uncompleted job in the workshop. The job card for this work can be summarised as follows.

Job costing sheet, Job no 487

Costs to date	£
Direct materials	1,025
Direct labour (120 hrs)	525
Production overhead (£3 per direct labour hour)	360
	1,910

A new job (job no. 488) was commenced in September. Production costs were as follows.

Direct materials	£
Issued to: job no. 487	3,585
Job no. 488	5,850
Damaged inventory written off from stores	3,450
	12,585

Material transfers	£
From job 487 to job 488	1,125
From job 487 to store	1,305

Direct labour	
Job no. 487	445 hrs
Job no. 488	280 hrs

The cost of labour hours in September was £4.50 per hour. Production overheads incurred during the month were £5,700.

The jobs were delivered to customers on completion, and invoiced as follows.

	£
Job 487	8,050
Job 488	12,000

Administration and marketing costs, which totalled £4,800 in September, are added to cost of sales at the rate of 20% of production cost.

Task

Using a spreadsheet package, prepare the summarised job cost cards for each job and calculate the profit on each completed job.

Activity 20

Vincent is drawing up his accounts for the year ended 31 December 20X7. He has extracted the following balances from his general ledger into the .spreadsheet **Ac_20_Q**, which you will find in your BPP data files.

	£
Fixtures and fittings at cost	21,650
Depreciation at 1 January 20X7	12,965
Motor vehicles at cost	37,628
Depreciation at 1 January 20X7	17,490
Inventory at 1 January 20X7	34,285
Debtors control account	91,440
Provision for doubtful debts	3,409
Cash in hand	361
Bank	14,297
Creditors control account	102,157
Revenue	354,291
Purchases	197,981
Wages and salaries	57,980
Rent and rates	31,650
Advertising	12,240
Administrative expenses	31,498
Bank charges	2,133
Bad debts written off	763
Equity	15,000

The following adjustments are required.

(a) Depreciation of fixtures and fittings at 20% on cost. Fittings with a cost of £1,880 are already fully written down.

(b) Depreciation of motor vehicles at 25% on cost. All cars are under three years old except for one (cost £7,640), which has a written down value of £1,146.

(c) Write-off of a specific debtor balance of £2,440. The provision is to be adjusted to 5% of debtors after this write-off.

(d) Closing inventory was valued at £37,238.

(e) An accrual has to be made for the fourth quarter's rent of £6,750.

(f) Sales made between Christmas and the New Year and for which invoices were mislaid for a couple of days (and so not posted) amounted to £4,300.

(g) Vincent wants to put in £10,000 of additional capital to be reflected in 20X7's accounts.

(h) Advertising costs include a prepayment of £500 per month for January to March 20X8.

(i) Bank charges of £508 have not been accrued.

Task

Using the information in the file **Ac_20_Q** Prepare an extended trial balance including final amounts for the profit and loss account and balance sheet.

Activity 21

Dittori Sage Ltd has a sales ledger package which does not offer an aged debtors option. You have decided to set up a simple spreadsheet to monitor ageing by region. You have been able to export the following information from the sales ledger, as at 31 May 20X6. This data is contained in a spreadsheet - file **Ac_21_Q** in your BPP data.

Invoices outstanding

Region	Current	1 month	2 month	3 month	4 month	5 month +
Highlands	346.60	567.84	32.17	-	-	54.80
Strathclyde	24,512.05	28,235.50	4,592.50	1,244.80	51.36	942.57
Borders	1,927.77	-	512.88	-	-	-
North West	824.80	14,388.91	2,473.53	-	482.20	79.66
North East	14,377.20	12,850.00	-	3,771.84	1,244.55	-
Midlands	45,388.27	61,337.88	24,001.02	4,288.31	1,391.27	4,331.11
Wales	14,318.91	5,473.53	21.99	4,881.64	512.27	422.50
East Anglia	157.20	943.68	377.40	1,500.87	15.33	247.66
South West	9,528.73	11,983.39	3,771.89	6,228.77	1,008.21	214.51
South East	68,110.78	83,914.54	29,117.96	24,285.10	14,328.90	5,422.50
France	6,422.80	7,451.47	5,897.55	2,103.70	140.50	3,228.76
Other EU	5,433.88	4,991.90	5,012.70	4,223.80	1,022.43	1,984.29
Rest of World	1,822.70	4,529.67	277.50	3,491.34	-	-

Task

Prepare a spreadsheet which will show the above analysis, total debtors by region and the percentage of debt in each category by region and in total.

Activity 22

A project will **cost** £1.5m (all incurred immediately) but it is expected to bring about net **savings** as follows.

	£		£
Year 1	271,000	Year 6	300,000
Year 2	226,000	Year 7	177,000
Year 3	249,000	Year 8	205,000
Year 4	275,000	Year 9	223,000
Year 5	265,000	Year 10	231,000

Task

Use a spreadsheet to perform NPV and IRR calculations to answer the following questions.

(a)   Determine whether the project should be undertaken if the rate of interest paid on a loan of £1.5m is 10%

(b)   It is possible that the rate of interest may increase to 11%. Should the project be undertaken if this happens?

(c)   What is the IRR of the project?

Activity 23

Open the spreadsheet file **Ac_23_Q** in your BPP data. You will see the following.

	A	B	C
1	2805TN		
2	1704VR		
3	3501OY		
4	9522CI		
5	8022LJ		
6	6865XY		
7	8506TZ		
8	1091UY		
9	7405RP		
10	5823PK		
11	9456RI		
12	3002QJ		
13	2567UO		
14	2805KM		
15	3309QI		
16	9324WU		
17	1675LW		
18	9941AU		
19	2673DO		
20	7833UH		
21	2769KD		
22	7484TS		
23	6433PE		

These are the first few of 1500 rows containing codes for materials used in your business. The numerical part of the code is your company's reference for the material. The alphabetic part refers to the supplier of the material.

Tasks

(a)   Sort all 1500 codes into **supplier** order (ie codes ending AA, codes ending AB, codes ending AC, etc). Use formulae. Do not retype any part of the code. Do not spend more than 5 minutes on this part of the task.

(b)   Do any of the codes appear more than once in the list? If so which ones? Again, do not spend more than five minutes trying to find out.

Activity 24

The following illustration shows a spreadsheet model for calculating depreciation of fixed assets on either a straight line basis or a reducing balance basis. The user enters figures in cells F3 to F6 and the model automatically calculates an annual depreciation charge, over up to 10 years.

The user enters the cost of the asset, the rate of depreciation, the method of depreciation ('s' for straight line; 'r' for reducing balance).

If the user wishes, there can also be a materiality level: a fixed asset will be written down to nil in the following year if the carried forward book value is lower than the materiality limit (if there is no materiality level, the user enters 0 in the Materiality cell).

Task

Devise a model like the one shown below.

	A	B	C	D	E	F	G	H	I	J	K
1											
2											
3					Cost	4599					
4					Rate	0.35					
5					Method	r					
6					Materiality	500					
7											
8											
9											
10											
11		Year 1	Year 2	Year 3	Year 4	Year 5	Year 6	Year 7	Year 8	Year 9	Year 10
12	NBV b/f	4599.00	2989.35	1943.08	1263.00	820.95	533.62	346.85	0.00	0.00	0.00
13	Depreciation	1609.65	1046.27	680.08	442.05	287.33	186.77	346.85	0.00	0.00	0.00
14	NBV c/f	2989.35	1943.08	1263.00	820.95	533.62	346.85	0.00	0.00	0.00	0.00
15											
16											

Answers to Practice Activities

Suggested solutions to the practice activities follow. There are often different ways to reach a satisfactory solution to an activity – you may have used a different approach but still completed the activity correctly.

Answer to Activity 1

The spreadsheet uses the LOOKUP function to match up the data in cell D3 with the corresponding data in cells C11 to C14. Cell D4 displays the value in the cell to the right of the cell in C11:C14 that matches the data in cell D3.

In other words if you tell the spreadsheet a person's name it looks up their age.

The formula used to do this is **=LOOKUP(D3,C11:D14)**

Answer to Activity 2

Look at the solution which is available in the file **Ac_02_S** This file will be on your hard drive in the in the folder C:\BPPTECH if you have installed the data files from the CD that accompanies this book.

Make sure you do not have your Caps Lock key on when you type the password. In this case you should type lower case letters only.

The total charge is £7,899.00.

The formula to use in column H is **=LOOKUP(F2,$A$2:$B$6)*G2**. You can then fill down the remaining rows and sum the column using the SUM function.

Answer to Activity 3

The solution is shown below.

The file is available as **Ac_03_S** in the folder where you are storing your BPP files.

	A	B	C	D	E	F	G	H	I	J	K	L
			Trial balance		Adjustments		Accrued	Prepaid	Revenue statement		Balance sheet	
1	**Dunraven**											
2	**ETB Year Ended 30/06/20X6**											
3	**Account**		Trial balance		Adjustments		Accrued	Prepaid	Revenue statement		Balance sheet	
4			£	£	£	£	£	£	£	£	£	£
5	Revenue	P		(336,247)					0	(336,247)	0	0
6	Purchases	P	224,362		1,624				225,986	0	0	0
7	Carriage	P	6,184			(1,624)			4,560	0	0	0
8	Drawings	B	14,686						0	0	14,686	0
9	Rent and rates	P	14,621				510	(2,120)	13,011	0	0	0
10	Postage and stationery	P	5,789						5,789	0	0	0
11	Advertising	P	2,941						2,941	0	0	0
12	Salaries and wages	P	56,934						56,934	0	0	0
13	Bad debt expense	P	1,614		256				1,870	0	0	0
14	Provision for Bad Debts	B		(365)		(256)			0	0	0	(621)
15	Debtors	B	31,050						0	0	31,050	0
16	Creditors	B		(9,456)					0	0	0	(9,456)
17	Cash in hand	B	422						0	0	422	0
18	Cash at bank	B	2,136						0	0	2,136	0
19	Inventory as at 1 July 20X5	P	15,605						15,605	0	0	0
20	Equipment	B	116,000						0	0	116,000	0
21	Depreciation	B		(55,400)		(17,400)			0	0	0	(72,800)
22	Equity	B		(90,876)					0	0	0	(90,876)
23	Prepayments	B					2,120		0	0	2,120	0
24	Accruals	B						(510)	0	0	0	(510)
25	Depreciation expense	P			17,400				17,400	0	0	0
26	Closing inventory	B			31,529				0	0	31,529	
27	Closing inventory	P				(31,529)			0	(31,529)	0	0
28									0	0	0	0
29												
30												
31	SUB-TOTAL		492,344	(492,344)	50,809	(50,809)	2,630	(2,630)	344,096	(367,776)	197,943	(174,263)
32	Profit for the year								23,680	0	0	(23,680)
33	**TOTAL**		492,344	(492,344)	50,809	(50,809)	2,630	(2,630)	367,776	(367,776)	197,943	(197,943)

Answer to Activity 4

The solution is shown below.

	A	B	C	D	E	F	G	H	I	J	K	L
1	Dunraven											
2	ETB Year Ended 30/06/20X6											
3	Account		Trial balance		Adjustments		Accrued	Prepaid	Revenue statement		Balance sheet	
4			£	£	£	£	£	£	£	£	£	£
5	Revenue	P		(336,247)					0	(336,247)	0	0
6	Purchases	P	224,362		1,624				225,986	0	0	0
7	Carriage	P	6,184			(1,624)			4,560	0	0	0
8	Drawings	B	14,686						0	0	14,686	0
9	Rent and rates	P	14,621				510	(2,120)	13,011	0	0	0
10	Postage and stationery	P	5,789						5,789	0	0	0
11	Advertising	P	2,941						2,941	0	0	0
12	Salaries and wages	P	56,934						56,934	0	0	0
13	Bad debt expense	P	1,614		256				1,870	0	0	0
14	Provision for Bad Debts	B		(365)		(256)			0	0	0	(621)
15	Debtors	B	31,050						0	0	31,050	0
16	Creditors	B		(9,456)					0	0	0	(9,456)
17	Cash in hand	B	422						0	0	422	0
18	Cash at bank	B	2,136						0	0	2,136	0
19	Inventory as at 1 July 20X5	P	15,605						15,605	0	0	0
20	Equipment	B	116,000						0	0	116,000	0
21	Depreciation	B		(55,400)		(23,200)			0	0	0	(78,600)
22	Equity	B		(90,876)					0	0	0	(90,876)
23	Prepaymets	B					2,120		0	0	2,120	0
24	Accruals	B						(510)	0	0	0	(510)
25	Depreciation expense	P			23,200				23,200	0	0	0
26	Closing inventory	B			31,529				0	0	31,529	0
27	Closing inventory	P				(31,529)			0	(31,529)	0	0
28									0	0	0	0
29												
30												
31	SUB-TOTAL		492,344	(492,344)	56,609	(56,609)	2,630	(2,630)	349,896	(367,776)	197,943	(180,063)
32	Profit for the year								17,880	0	0	(17,880)
33	TOTAL		492,344	(492,344)	56,609	(56,609)	2,630	(2,630)	367,776	(367,776)	197,943	(197,943)

Answer to Activity 5

The solution follows.

	A	B	C	D	E	F	G	H	I	J	K	L
1	Oaklands											
2	ETB Year Ended 30/06/20X4											
3	Account		Trial balance		Adjustments		Accrued	Prepaid	Revenue statement		Balance sheet	
4			£	£	£	£	£	£	£	£	£	£
5												
6	Equity	B		(44,550)					0	0	0	(44,550)
7	Freehold L & B	B	25,000						0	0	25,000	0
8	F & F: cost	B	3,360						0	0	3,360	0
9	F&F: depn	B		(2,016)		(336)			0	0	0	(2,352)
10	MV: cost	B	1,900						0	0	1,900	0
11	MV: depn	B		(980)		(380)			0	0	0	(1,360)
12	Purchases	P	101,286						101,286	0	0	0
13	Revenue	P		(142,125)					0	(142,125)	0	0
14	Rent received	P		(810)		(268)			0	(1,078)	0	0
15	Drawings	B	9,732						0	0	9,732	0
16	Car expenses	P	841						841	0	0	0
17	Inventory as at 1/1/20X4	P	10,858						10,858	0	0	0
18	Bad debt expense	P	943			(147)			796	0	0	0
19	Prov' doubtful debts 1/1/20X4	B		(792)	147				0	0	0	(645)
20	General expenses	P	1,842					(86)	1,756	0	0	0
21	Rent and rates	P	2,414					(106)	2,308	0	0	0
22	Trade Debtors	B	16,121						0	0	16,121	0
23	Trade Creditors	B		(9,125)					0	0	0	(9,125)
24	Wages and salaries	P	18,103			0	421		18,524	0	0	0
25	Discounts allowed	P	3,125						3,125	0	0	0
26	Bank	B	4,873						0	0	4,873	0
27	Inventory as at 31/12/20X4	B			12,654				0	0	12,654	0
28	Inventory as at 31/12/20X4	P				(12,654)			0	(12,654)	0	0
29	Accruals	B						(421)	0	0	0	(421)
30	Prepayments	B					192		0	0	192	0
31	Depreciation expense	P			716				716	0	0	0
32	Sundry debtors	B			268				0	0	268	0
33												
34												
35	SUB-TOTAL		200,398	(200,398)	13,785	(13,785)	613	(613)	140,210	(155,857)	74,100	(58,453)
36	Retained earnings for the year								15,647	0	0	(15,647)
37	TOTAL		200,398	(200,398)	13,785	(13,785)	613	(613)	155,857	(155,857)	74,100	(74,100)

Answer to Activity 6

The solution to Activity 6 is shown below.

The formula we used to amend the depreciation provision was =-(C10+D11)*0.25

	A	B	C	D	E	F	G	H	I	J	K	_
1	Oaklands											
2	ETB Year Ended 30/06/20X4											
3	Account		Trial balance		Adjustments		Accrued	Prepaid	Revenue statement		Balance sheet	
4			£	£	£	£	£	£	£	£	£	£
5												
6	Equity	B		(44,550)					0	0	0	(44,550)
7	Freehold L & B	B	25,000						0	0	25,000	0
8	F & F: cost	B	3,360						0	0	3,360	0
9	F&F: depn	B		(2,016)		(336)			0	0	0	(2,352)
10	MV: cost	B	1,900						0	0	1,900	0
11	MV: depn	B		(980)		(230)			0	0	0	(1,210)
12	Purchases	P	101,286						101,286	0	0	0
13	Revenue	P		(142,125)					0	(142,125)	0	0
14	Rent received	P		(810)		(268)			0	(1,078)	0	0
15	Drawings	B	9,732						0	0	9,732	0
16	Car expenses	P	841						841	0	0	0
17	Inventory as at 1/1/20X4	P	10,858						10,858	0	0	0
18	Bad debt expense	P	943			(147)			796	0	0	0
19	Prov' doubtful debts 1/1/20X4	B		(792)	147				0	0	0	(645)
20	General expenses	P	1,842					(86)	1,756	0	0	0
21	Rent and rates	P	2,414					(106)	2,308	0	0	0
22	Trade Debtors	B	16,121						0	0	16,121	0
23	Trade Creditors	B		(9,125)					0	0	0	(9,125)
24	Wages and salaries	P	18,103			0	421		18,524	0	0	0
25	Discounts allowed	P	3,125						3,125	0	0	0
26	Bank	B	4,873						0	0	4,873	0
27	Inventory as at 31/12/20X4	B			12,654				0	0	12,654	0
28	Inventory as at 31/12/20X4	P				(12,654)			0	(12,654)	0	0
29	Accruals	B						(421)	0	0	0	(421)
30	Prepayments	B					192		0	0	192	0
31	Depreciation expense	P			566				566	0	0	0
32	Sundry debtors	B			268				0	0	268	0
33												
34												
35	SUB-TOTAL		200,398	(200,398)	13,635	(13,635)	613	(613)	140,060	(155,857)	74,100	(58,303)
36	Retained earnings for the year								15,797	0	0	(15,797)
37	TOTAL		200,398	(200,398)	13,635	(13,635)	613	(613)	155,857	(155,857)	74,100	(74,100)

Answer to Activity 7

Here are the formulae.

	A	B	C	D
1	36945	=DAY(A1)	=MONTH(A1)	=YEAR(A1)
2	37256	=DAY(A2)	=MONTH(A2)	=YEAR(A2)
3	=A2-A1			

The dates in column A have been formatted (using the custom option) as dd/mm/yyyy. Subtracting dates from one another shows the number of days between the two dates, in this case 311.

Answer to Activity 8

A full solution is shown below, followed by an illustration showing the formulae used in the spreadsheet.

	A	B	C	D	E	F
1	**Goodwood Furniture**					
2	**Overhead apportionment**					
3	*Budget*					
4						
5						
6	*Total overheads*					
7		£				
8	Rent and rates	12,800				
9	Machine insurance	6,000				
10	Telephone charges	3,200				
11	Depreciation	18,000				
12	Production supervisor	24,000				
13	Heat and light	6,400				
14		70,400				
15						
16	*Departmental statistics*					
17		*Dept A*	*Dept B*	*Dept C*	*Dept X*	*Dept Y*
18	Floor area (sq. m)	3,000	1,800	600	600	400
19	Machine value (£)	24,000	10,000	8,000	4,000	2,000
20	Direct labour hours	3,200	1,800	1,000		
21	Labour rates/hour (£)	3.80	3.50	3.40	3.00	3.00
22						
23	*Allocated overheads*					
24		*Dept A*	*Dept B*	*Dept C*		
25	Specific to each department	2,800	1,700	1,200	800	600
26	Apportionment of costs of Dept	50%	25%	25%		
27	Apportionment of costs of Dept	20%	30%	50%		
28						
29	**Apportionment calculation**					
30	*Overhead*					
31		*Dept A*	*Dept B*	*Dept C*	*Dept X*	*Dept Y*
32	Costs specific to each dept	2,800	1,700	1,200	800	600
33	Rent and rates	6000	3600	1200	1200	800
34	Machine insurance	3000	1250	1000	500	250
35	Telephone charges	1500	900	300	300	200
36	Depreciation	9000	3750	3000	1500	750
37	Production supervisor	12800	7200	4000		
38	Heat and light	3000	1800	600	600	400
39		38,100	20,200	11,300	4,900	3,000
40	Apportionment of costs of Dept	2450	1225	1225		
41	Apportionment of costs of Dept	600	900	1500		
42		41,150	22,325	14,025		
43						
44	**Absorption rate**					
45		*Dept A*	*Dept B*	*Dept C*		
46		£	£	£		
47	Rate per labour hour	12.86	12.40	14.03		
48						

	A	B	C	D	E	F
1	**Goodwood Furniture**					
2	**Overhead apportionment**					
3	*Budget*					
4						
28						
29	**Apportionment calculation**					
30	*Overhead*					
31		*Dept A*	*Dept B*	*Dept C*	*Dept X*	*Dept Y*
32	Costs specific to each dept	=B25	=C25	=D25	=E25	=F25
33	Rent and rates	=B8*B18/SUM(B18:F18)	=B8*C18/SUM(B18:F18)	=B8*D18/SUM(B18:F18)	=B8*E18/SUM(B18:F18)	=B8*F18/SUM(B18:F18)
34	Machine insurance	=B9*B19/SUM(B19:F19)	=B9*C19/SUM(B19:F19)	=B9*D19/SUM(B19:F19)	=B9*E19/SUM(B19:F19)	=B9*F19/SUM(B19:F19)
35	Telephone charges	=B10*B18/SUM(B18:F18)	=B10*C18/SUM(B18:F18)	=B10*D18/SUM(B18:F18)	=B10*E18/SUM(B18:F18)	=B10*F18/SUM(B18:F18)
36	Depreciation	=B11*B19/SUM(B19:F19)	=B11*C19/SUM(B19:F19)	=B11*D19/SUM(B19:F19)	=B11*E19/SUM(B19:F19)	=B11*F19/SUM(B19:F19)
37	Production supervisor	=B12*B20/SUM(B20:D20)	=B12*C20/SUM(B20:D20)	=B12*D20/SUM(B20:D20)		
38	Heat and light	=B13*B18/SUM(B18:F18)	=B13*C18/SUM(B18:F18)	=B13*D18/SUM(B18:F18)	=B13*E18/SUM(B18:F18)	=B13*F18/SUM(B18:F18)
39		=SUM(B32:B38)	=SUM(C32:C38)	=SUM(D32:D38)	=SUM(E32:E38)	=SUM(F32:F38)
40	Apportionment of costs of Dept X	=E39*B26	=E39*C26	=E39*D26		
41	Apportionment of costs of Dept Y	=F39*B27	=F39*C27	=F39*D27		
42		=SUM(B39:B41)	=SUM(C39:C41)	=SUM(D39:D41)		
43						
44	**Absorption rate**					
45		*Dept A*	*Dept B*	*Dept C*		
46		£	£	£		
47	Rate per labour hour	=B42/B20	=C42/C20	=D42/D20		
48						

Answer to Activity 9

The spreadsheet would appear as follows. In this situation you could use cells as a 'calculator', for example, cell B8 could be changed from 12,800 to =12,800*1.05, and so on.

Better (and you should now be firmly in the habit of never mixing up cell references and 'real' numbers in formulae), is to copy the values in cells B8 to B13 into cells D8 to D13, enter the changes (1.05, 1.10 etc) in cells C8 to C13, and then change the values in B8 to B13 to formulae:=C8*D8 and so on. This would be the 'Advanced' answer, so well done if you got this.

	A	B	C	D	E	F
1	Goodwood Furniture					
2	Overhead apportionment					
3	Budget					
4						
5		1.05				
6	Total overheads					
7		£	Change	Revised		
8	Rent and rates	13,440	1.05	12,800		
9	Machine insurance	6,600	1.10	6,000		
10	Telephone charges	4,000	1.25	3,200		
11	Depreciation	18,000	1	18,000		
12	Production supervisor	24,672	1.028	24,000		
13	Heat and light	5,888	0.92	6,400		
14		72,600		70,400		
15						
16	Departmental statistics					
17		Dept A	Dept B	Dept C	Dept X	Dept Y
18	Floor area (sq. m)	3,000	1,800	600	600	400
19	Machine value (£)	24,000	10,000	8,000	4,000	2,000
20	Direct labour hours	3,200	1,800	1,000		
21	Labour rates/hour (£)	3.80	3.50	3.40	3.00	3.00
22						
23	Allocated overheads					
24		Dept A	Dept B	Dept C		
25	Specific to each department	2,800	1,700	1,200	800	600
26	Apportionment of costs of Dept	50%	25%	25%		
27	Apportionment of costs of Dept	20%	30%	50%		
28						
29	Apportionment calculation					
30	Overhead					
31		Dept A	Dept B	Dept C	Dept X	Dept Y
32	Costs specific to each dept	2,800	1,700	1,200	800	600
33	Rent and rates	6300	3780	1260	1260	840
34	Machine insurance	3300	1375	1100	550	275
35	Telephone charges	1875	1125	375	375	250
36	Depreciation	9000	3750	3000	1500	750
37	Production supervisor	13158.4	7401.6	4112		
38	Heat and light	2760	1656	552	552	368
39		39,193	20,788	11,599	5,037	3,083
40	Apportionment of costs of Dept	2518.5	1259.25	1259.25		
41	Apportionment of costs of Dept	616.6	924.9	1541.5		
42		42,329	22,972	14,400		
43						
44	Absorption rate					
45		Dept A	Dept B	Dept C		
46		£	£	£		
47	Rate per labour hour	13.23	12.76	14.40		
48						

BPP
PROFESSIONAL EDUCATION

Answer to Activity 10

The spreadsheet is available as **Ac_10_S** in the folder where you are storing your BPP files.

Cell A18 should contain the formula =B14. The row variable is B8 and the column variable is B3. The figures are as follows. Reading from the table the net profit in the circumstances described will be £16,875.

	A	B	C	D	E	F	G	H
1								
2	Standard fee £	300						
3	Number of clients	100						
4	Average time (hours)	5						
5	Variable costs per hour (£)	20		Fee income formula **isn't**				
6	Fixed costs per annum (£)	5,000		affected by the variability				
7				index as jobs are charged out				
8	Variability index	1.00		at a flat rate				
9				=B2*B3				
10		£						
11	Fee income	30,000		The variable cost formula **is**				
12	Variable costs	(10,000)		affected by the variability index:				
13	Fixed costs	(5,000)		=-(B5*B4*B3)*B8				
14	Net profit	15,000						
15								
16								
17								
18	15,000	0.50	0.75	1.00	1.25	1.50	1.75	2.00
19	0	(5,000)	(5,000)	(5,000)	(5,000)	(5,000)	(5,000)	(5,000)
20	25	1,250	625	0	(625)	(1,250)	(1,875)	(2,500)
21	50	7,500	6,250	5,000	3,750	2,500	1,250	0
22	75	13,750	11,875	10,000	8,125	6,250	4,375	2,500
23	100	20,000	17,500	15,000	12,500	10,000	7,500	5,000
24	125	26,250	23,125	20,000	16,875	13,750	10,625	7,500
25	150	32,500	28,750	25,000	21,250	17,500	13,750	10,000
26	200	45,000	40,000	35,000	30,000	25,000	20,000	15,000
27	225	51,250	45,625	40,000	34,375	28,750	23,125	17,500
28	250	57,500	51,250	45,000	38,750	32,500	26,250	20,000
29								
30				The net profit when 125 jobs are taken				
31				with a difficulty weighting of 1.25				
32								

Answer to Activity 11

The answer shown below is available as the file **Ac_11_S** in the BPP data files.

	A	B	C	D	E	F
1		International Magazines Limited: Sales by Region Jan-Jun 2003				
2		Europe	America	Rest of the world	Total	
3	Woman's Day	251,208	163,514	105,000	£ 519,722	
4	Blue!	202,262	136,290	78,485	£ 417,036	
5	Easy Cooking	143,588	86,040	114,900	£ 344,528	
6	Sorted!	27,795	6,234	14,769	£ 48,798	
7	Total	£ 624,852	£ 392,078	£ 313,154	£ 1,330,083	
8						
9						
10						
11						
12						

Sales by magazine and region Jan-Jun 2003

Answer to Activity 12

We strongly encourage you to learn how to use the Pivot Table facility. It is on of the most widely used spreadsheet functions. A spreadsheet that has a Pivot Table in it already may be found in the file **Ac_12_S**

To have a look at how this has been set up you can right click with your mouse in a cell in the Pivot Table. A menu like the following menu will appear. Select the **Wizard ...** option and you will be taken back to the layout stage of the Pivot Table production process.

	A	B	C	D	E	F	G
1	Sum of Quantity	Colour					
2	Shape	Blue	Green	Red	Yellow	Grand Total	
3	Round	482	584	297	824	2187	
4	Square	628	1440	1240	1153	4461	
5	Triangular	1195	1139	1114	7		
6	Grand Total	2305	3163	2651	27		
7							
8							
9							
10							
11							
12							
13							
14							
15							
16							
17							
18							
19							
20							

Menu overlay:
- Format Cells...
- Insert
- Delete
- Wizard...
- Refresh Data
- Select ▶
- Group and Outline ▶
- Formulas ▶
- Field...
- Options...
- Show Pages...

Answer to Activity 13

(a) and (b)

We have set up the balance sheet and income statement as part of the spreadsheet. This means that any changes, for example to the opening balance sheet, can be included with minimal re-input.

(c) to (i) The variables to be entered are as follows.

	A	B	C	D	E
28					
29	**Opening B/Sheet**	£'000			
30	Land and buildings	220			
31	Plant and machinery	110			
32	Motor vehicles	65			
33	Stock	40			
34	Trade debtors	60			
35	Cash in hand	5			
36	Overdraft	-65			
37	Trade creditors	-35			
38	Long term creditors	-120			
39		=SUM(B30:B38)			
40					
41	**Income statement**	£'000	July	Aug	Sept
42	Sales	390	=$B$42*B53	=$B$42*B53	=$B$42*$B$54
43	Purchases	-165	=$B$43/12		
44	Rent and rates	-60			
45	Depreciation	-30			
46	Marketing	-35			
47	Administrative expenses	-75			
48	Selling expenses	-45			
49	Profit/loss before interest	=SUM(B42:B48)			
50					
51					
52	**Other data required**				
53	Sales July/August	=1/6			
54	Sales other months	=(1-(2*B53))/10			
55	Debtor collection (Mth 0)	0.1			
56	Debtor collection (Mth 1)	0.6			
57	Debtor collection (Mth 2)	0.3			
58	Opening debtors collection	0.9			
59	Creditors payment (Mth 0)	0.2			
60	Creditors payment (Mth 1)	0.8			
61	Rates	-20			
62	Rent per quarter	=(B44-B61)/4			
63	Marketing per month	-1			
64	Marketing burst (Nov)	=B46-(11*B63)			
65	Admin expenses	=B47/12			
66	Monthly interest rate (o'draft)	0.02			
67					

The results are shown in the following illustration.

	A	B	C	D	E	F	G	H	I	J	K	L	M	N
1	Rolling Projections Ltd													
2	Cash flow forecast													
3	Year ending 30 June 20X6	July	Aug	Sept	Oct	Nov	Dec	Jan	Feb	Mar	April	May	June	Total
4		£'000	£'000	£'000	£'000	£'000	£'000	£'000	£'000	£'000	£'000	£'000	£'000	£'000
5	Cash inflows													
6	Opening debtors	54.00												54.00
7	Month of sale	6.50	6.50	2.60	2.60	2.60	2.60	2.60	2.60	2.60	2.60	2.60	2.60	39.00
8	1 month		39.00	39.00	15.60	15.60	15.60	15.60	15.60	15.60	15.60	15.60	15.60	218.40
9	2 months			19.50	19.50	7.80	7.80	7.80	7.80	7.80	7.80	7.80	7.80	101.40
10	Total receipts	60.50	45.50	61.10	37.70	26.00	26.00	26.00	26.00	26.00	26.00	26.00	26.00	412.80
11														
12	Cash outflows													
13	Opening creditors		-35.00											-35.00
14	Month of purchase	-2.75	-2.75	-2.75	-2.75	-2.75	-2.75	-2.75	-2.75	-2.75	-2.75	-2.75	-2.75	-33.00
15	1 month		-11.00	-11.00	-11.00	-11.00	-11.00	-11.00	-11.00	-11.00	-11.00	-11.00	-11.00	-121.00
16	Rent			-10.00			-10.00			-10.00			-10.00	-40.00
17	Rates										-20.00			-20.00
18	Marketing	-1.00	-1.00	-1.00	-1.00	-24.00	-1.00	-1.00	-1.00	-1.00	-1.00	-1.00	-1.00	-35.00
19	Administrative expenses	-6.25	-6.25	-6.25	-6.25	-6.25	-6.25	-6.25	-6.25	-6.25	-6.25	-6.25	-6.25	-75.00
20	Selling expenses	-7.50	-7.50	-3.00	-3.00	-3.00	-3.00	-3.00	-3.00	-3.00	-3.00	-3.00	-3.00	-45.00
21	Total payments	-17.50	-63.50	-34.00	-24.00	-47.00	-34.00	-24.00	-24.00	-34.00	-44.00	-24.00	-34.00	-404.00
22														
23	Net cash flow	43.00	-18.00	27.10	13.70	-21.00	-8.00	2.00	2.00	-8.00	-18.00	2.00	-8.00	8.80
24	Blance b/f	-65.00	-22.44	-41.25	-14.43	-0.75	-22.18	-30.78	-29.36	-27.91	-36.63	-55.72	-54.79	-65.00
25	Balance c/f (pre Interest)	-22.00	-40.44	-14.15	-0.73	-21.75	-30.18	-28.78	-27.36	-35.91	-54.63	-53.72	-62.79	-56.20
26	Interest	-0.44	-0.81	-0.28	-0.01	-0.43	-0.60	-0.58	-0.55	-0.72	-1.09	-1.07	-1.26	-7.85
27	Balance c/f (post Interest)	-22.44	-41.25	-14.43	-0.75	-22.18	-30.78	-29.36	-27.91	-36.63	-55.72	-54.79	-64.05	-64.05
28														

The formulae we used are shown in the extract below.

	A	B	C	D	E	F
1	Rolling Projections Lt					
2	Cash flow forecast					
3	Year ending 30 June	July	Aug	Sept	Oct	Nov
4		£'000	£'000	£'000	£'000	£'000
5	Cash inflows					
6	Opening debtors	=$B$34*B58				
7	Month of sale	=C42*$B$55	=D42*$B$55	=$E$42*$B$55	=$E$42*$B$55	=$E$42*$B$55
8	1 month		=C42*$B$56	=D42*$B$56	=$E$42*$B$56	=$E$42*$B$56
9	2 months			=C42*$B$57	=D42*$B$57	=$E$42*$B$57
10	Total receipts	=SUM(B6:B9)	=SUM(C6:C9)	=SUM(D6:D9)	=SUM(E6:E9)	=SUM(F6:F9)
11						
12	Cash outflows					
13	Opening creditors		=B37			
14	Month of purchase	=$C$43*$B$59	=$C$43*$B$59	=$C$43*$B$59	=$C$43*$B$59	=$C$43*$B$59
15	1 month		=$C$43*$B$60	=$C$43*$B$60	=$C$43*$B$60	=$C$43*$B$60
16	Rent			=B62		
17	Rates					
18	Marketing	=$B$63	=$B$63	=$B$63	=$B$63	=B64
19	Administrative expenses	=$B$65	=$B$65	=$B$65	=$B$65	=$B$65
20	Selling expenses	=$B$48*$B$53	=$B$48*$B$53	=$B$48*$B$54	=$B$48*$B$54	=$B$48*$B$54
21	Total payments	=SUM(B13:B20)	=SUM(C13:C20)	=SUM(D13:D20)	=SUM(E13:E20)	=SUM(F13:F20)
22						
23	Net cash flow	=B10+B21	=C10+C21	=D10+D21	=E10+E21	=F10+F21
24	Balance b/f	=B36	=B27	=C27	=D27	=E27
25	Balance c/f (pre Interest)	=SUM(B23:B24)	=SUM(C23:C24)	=SUM(D23:D24)	=SUM(E23:E24)	=SUM(F23:F24)
26	Interest	=IF(B25<0,B25*$B$66,0)	=IF(C25<0,C25*$B$66,0)	=IF(D25<0,D25*$B$66,0)	=IF(E25<0,E25*$B$66,0)	=IF(F25<0,F25*$B$66,0)
27	Balance c/f (post Interest)	=SUM(B25:B26)	=SUM(C25:C26)	=SUM(D25:D26)	=SUM(E25:E26)	=SUM(F25:F26)
28						

Answer to Activity 14

We have tackled this by inserting five rows immediately beneath the relevant section of the spreadsheet. (This does not affect the lower part of the spreadsheet - check the formulae for yourself.)

	A	B	C	D	E	F	G	H	I	J	K	L	M	N
27	Balance c/f (post Interest)	-22.44	-41.25	-14.43	-0.75	-22.18	-30.78	-29.36	-27.91	-36.63	-55.72	-54.79	-64.05	-64.05
28														
29	**Overdraft facility**													
30	Amount of facility	-50.00												
31	Faciltiy exceeded?	No	No	No	No	No	No	No	No	No	Yes	Yes	Yes	
32	Headroom/(excess)	27.56	8.75	35.57	49.25	27.82	19.22	20.64	22.09	13.37	-5.72	-4.79	-14.05	

The formulae we used are shown below. They have been copied right across to the June column.

	A	B	C	D	
27	Balance c/f (post Interest)	=SUM(B25:B26)	=SUM(C25:C26)	=SUM(D25:D26)	:
28					
29	**Overdraft facility**				
30	Amount of facility	-50			
31	Faciltiy exceeded?	=IF($B$30>B27, "Yes", "No")	=IF($B$30>C27, "Yes", "No")	=IF($B$30>D27, "Yes", "No")	:
32	Headroom/(excess)	=B27-$B$30	=C27-$B$30	=D27-$B$30	:

Answer to Activity 15

(a)   The 'skeleton' spreadsheet is shown below. We decided it was more logical to present the earliest material on the left - and work from left to right with time.

	A	B	C	D	E	F
1	**Special assignment**					
2	Personnel Costs					
3		**Week 1**	**Week 2**	**Week 3**	**Total**	
4		Cost	Cost	Cost	Cost	
5		£	£	£	£	
6	Divisional chief accountant	0.00	0.00	0.00	0.00	
7	Assistant accountant	0.00	0.00	0.00	0.00	
8	Accounting technician	0.00	0.00	0.00	0.00	
9	Secretary	0.00	0.00	0.00	0.00	
10	Total cost	0.00	0.00	0.00	0.00	
11						
12		Hours	Hours	Hours	Hours	
13	Divisional chief accountant				0.00	
14	Assistant accountant				0.00	
15	Accounting technician				0.00	
16	Secretary				0.00	
17	Total	0.00	0.00	0.00	0.00	
18						
19	*Chargeout rates*					
20	Divisional chief accountant	72.50	72.50	72.50		
21	Assistant accountant	38.00	38.00	38.00		
22	Accounting technician	21.45	21.45	21.45		
23	Secretary	17.30	17.30	17.30		

The underlying formulae are as follows.

	A	B	C	D	E
1	**Special assignment**				
2	Personnel Costs				
3		**Week 1**	**Week 2**	**Week 3**	**Total**
4		Cost	Cost	Cost	Cost
5		£	£	£	£
6	Divisional chief accountant	=B13*B20	=C13*C20	=D13*D20	=SUM(B6:D6)
7	Assistant accountant	=B14*B21	=C14*C21	=D14*D21	=SUM(B7:D7)
8	Accounting technician	=B15*B22	=C15*C22	=D15*D22	=SUM(B8:D8)
9	Secretary	=B16*B23	=C16*C23	=D16*D23	=SUM(B9:D9)
10	Total cost	=SUM(B6:B9)	=SUM(C6:C9)	=SUM(D6:D9)	=SUM(E6:E9)
11					
12		Hours	Hours	Hours	Hours
13	Divisional chief accountant				=SUM(B13:D13)
14	Assistant accountant				=SUM(B14:D14)
15	Accounting technician				=SUM(B15:D15)
16	Secretary				=SUM(B16:D16)
17	Total	=SUM(B13:B16)	=SUM(C13:C16)	=SUM(D13:D16)	=SUM(E13:E16)
18					
19	*Chargeout rates*				
20	Divisional chief accountant	72.5	=$B20	=$B20	
21	Assistant accountant	38	=$B21	=$B21	
22	Accounting technician	21.45	=$B22	=$B22	
23	Secretary	17.3	=$B23	=$B23	
24					

(b)   The final spreadsheet is shown below.

	A	B	C	D	E
1	**Special assignment**				
2	Personnel Costs				
3		**Week 1**	**Week 2**	**Week 3**	**Total**
4		Cost	Cost	Cost	Cost
5		£	£	£	£
6	Divisional chief accountant	0.00	326.25	489.38	815.63
7	Assistant accountant	760.00	1520.00	1330.00	3610.00
8	Accounting technician	686.40	858.00	804.38	2348.78
9	Secretary	259.50	556.54	644.43	1460.47
10	Total cost	1705.90	3260.79	3268.18	8234.87
11					
12		Hours	Hours	Hours	Hours
13	Divisional chief accountant	0.00	4.50	6.75	11.25
14	Assistant accountant	20.00	40.00	35.00	95.00
15	Accounting technician	32.00	40.00	37.50	109.50
16	Secretary	15.00	32.17	37.25	84.42
17	Total	67.00	116.67	116.50	300.17
18					
19	*Chargeout rates*				
20	Divisional chief accountant	72.50	72.50	72.50	
21	Assistant accountant	38.00	38.00	38.00	
22	Accounting technician	21.45	21.45	21.45	
23	Secretary	17.30	17.30	17.30	
24					

Answer to Activity 16

Before you can input any of the new data, you need to amend the design of the spreadsheet by inserting a column for week 4, altering your SUM formulae as necessary, adding extra lines for the laptops and taking account of the chargeout rate change. (We have treated a laptop unit as a single 40-hour unit; you might have chosen to allocate 40 one-hour units to each.)

The revised spreadsheet before data entry follows. It is important to design a spreadsheet such as this in a way that enables future modifications to be made as easily as possible.

	A	B	C	D	E	F
1	**Special assignment**					
2	Costs					
3		**Week 1**	**Week 2**	**Week 3**	**Week 4**	**Total**
4		Cost	Cost	Cost	Cost	Cost
5	*Personnel*	£	£	£	£	£
6	Divisional chief accountant	=B15*B25	=C15*C25	=D15*D25	=E15*E25	=SUM(B6:E6)
7	Assistant accountant	=B16*B26	=C16*C26	=D16*D26	=E16*E26	=SUM(B7:E7)
8	Accounting technician	=B17*B27	=C17*C27	=D17*D27	=E17*E27	=SUM(B8:E8)
9	Secretary	=B18*B28	=C18*C28	=D18*D28	=E18*E28	=SUM(B9:E9)
10	Total personnel cost	=SUM(B6:B9)	=SUM(C6:C9)	=SUM(D6:D9)		=SUM(F6:F9)
11	Cost of laptops	=B22*B29	=C22*C29	=D22*D29	=E22*E29	=SUM(B11:E11)
12	Total cost	=SUM(B6:B11)	=SUM(C6:C11)	=SUM(D6:D11)	=SUM(E6:E11)	=SUM(F10:F11)
13						
14	*Personnel*	Hours	Hours	Hours	Hours	Hours
15	Divisional chief accountant	0	4.5	6.75	6	=SUM(B15:E15)
16	Assistant accountant	20	40	35	0	=SUM(B16:E16)
17	Accounting technician	32	40	37.5	0	=SUM(B17:E17)
18	Secretary	15	32.17	37.25	0	=SUM(B18:E18)
19	Total	=SUM(B15:B18)	=SUM(C15:C18)	=SUM(D15:D18)	=SUM(E15:E18)	=SUM(F15:F18)
20						
21	*Laptops*	No	No	No	No	
22		2	2	2		
23						
24	*Chargeout rates*					
25	Divisional chief accountant	72.5	=$B25	=$B25	=$B25	
26	Assistant accountant	38	=$B26	=$B26	=$B26	
27	Accounting technician	21.45	=$B27	=$B27	=$B27	
28	Secretary	17.3	=$B28	=$B28*1.1	=$B28*1.1	
29	Laptops	100	=$B29	=$B29	=$B29	
30						
31						

67

The final spreadsheet is shown below.

	A	B	C	D	E	F
1	**Special assignment**					
2	Costs					
3		**Week 1**	**Week 2**	**Week 3**	**Week 4**	**Total**
4		Cost	Cost	Cost	Cost	Cost
5	*Personnel*	£	£	£	£	£
6	Divisional chief accountant	0.00	326.25	489.38	435.00	1250.63
7	Assistant accountant	760.00	1520.00	1330.00	0.00	3610.00
8	Accounting technician	686.40	858.00	804.38	0.00	2348.78
9	Secretary	259.50	556.54	708.87	0.00	1524.91
10	Total personnel cost	1705.9	3260.79	3332.62	435.00	8734.3085
11	Cost of laptops	200	200	200	0	600
12	Total cost	1905.90	3460.79	3532.62	435.00	9334.31
13						
14	*Personnel*	Hours	Hours	Hours	Hours	Hours
15	Divisional chief accountant	0.00	4.50	6.75	6.00	17.25
16	Assistant accountant	20.00	40.00	35.00	0.00	95.00
17	Accounting technician	32.00	40.00	37.50	0.00	109.50
18	Secretary	15.00	32.17	37.25	0.00	84.42
19	Total	67.00	116.67	116.50	6.00	306.17
20						
21	*Laptops*	No	No	No	No	
22		2	2	2	0	
23						

Answer to Activity 17

We adopted the following approach.

(a)   Inclusion of appropriate titles and column headings. We have included a 'Sundry' column for each of the payments *and* receipts.

(b)   Inclusion of additional columns for entry of narrative, date and reference of the user's choice (eg to show where the b/f entry comes from).

(c)   Once-only entry of each transaction in the appropriate analysed column. This is then *automatically* taken to the receipts or payments column as appropriate and then a new total inserted.

(d)   To prevent zeros being displayed all down columns E and H, we selected Tools and then Options and turned off the display of zero values.

(e)   To prevent totals being displayed all down column N, we used a conditional function to ensure that totals are only displayed as far down the page as the entries have been made. We have assumed that, because only a payment or a receipt is entered on a single line, if payments and receipts are equal, they must both equal zero and therefore have no entries. This will become clear if you try it out.

(f)   To prevent accidental or deliberate manipulation of the page, we selected Tools and then Protect Sheet, having first ensured that cell protection had been switched off (unlocked) for the following cells through the Format Cell..menu.

A9-B28

D9-D28

F9-G28

I9-M28

F2-F3

Our spreadsheet is shown below. This is available in the file **Ac_17_S**

	A	B	C	D	E	F	G	H	I	J	K	L	M	N
1	Bright Ideas Ltd													
2	Petty cash				Week number:									
3					Week ending:									
4														
5														
6	Narrative	Date	Line	Ref	Receipts	Sales	Sundry	Payments	Postage	Static	Kitch	Gifts	Sund	Balance
7					£	£	£	£	£	£	£	£	£	£
8	Balance b/f													
9			1		=F9+G9			=SUM(I9:M9)						=IF(E9=H9,0,N8+E9-H9)
10			2		=F10+G10			=SUM(I10:M10)						=IF(E10=H10,0,N9+E10-H10)
11			3		=F11+G11			=SUM(I11:M11)						=IF(E11=H11,0,N10+E11-H11)
12			4		=F12+G12			=SUM(I12:M12)						=IF(E12=H12,0,N11+E12-H12)
13			5		=F13+G13			=SUM(I13:M13)						=IF(E13=H13,0,N12+E13-H13)
14			6		=F14+G14			=SUM(I14:M14)						=IF(E14=H14,0,N13+E14-H14)
15			7		=F15+G15			=SUM(I15:M15)						=IF(E15=H15,0,N14+E15-H15)
16			8		=F16+G16			=SUM(I16:M16)						=IF(E16=H16,0,N15+E16-H16)
17			9		=F17+G17			=SUM(I17:M17)						=IF(E17=H17,0,N16+E17-H17)
18			10		=F18+G18			=SUM(I18:M18)						=IF(E18=H18,0,N17+E18-H18)
19			11		=F19+G19			=SUM(I19:M19)						=IF(E19=H19,0,N18+E19-H19)
20			12		=F20+G20			=SUM(I20:M20)						=IF(E20=H20,0,N19+E20-H20)
21			13		=F21+G21			=SUM(I21:M21)						=IF(E21=H21,0,N20+E21-H21)
22			14		=F22+G22			=SUM(I22:M22)						=IF(E22=H22,0,N21+E22-H22)
23			15		=F23+G23			=SUM(I23:M23)						=IF(E23=H23,0,N22+E23-H23)
24			16		=F24+G24			=SUM(I24:M24)						=IF(E24=H24,0,N23+E24-H24)
25			17		=F25+G25			=SUM(I25:M25)						=IF(E25=H25,0,N24+E25-H25)
26			18		=F26+G26			=SUM(I26:M26)						=IF(E26=H26,0,N25+E26-H26)
27			19		=F27+G27			=SUM(I27:M27)						=IF(E27=H27,0,N26+E27-H27)
28			20		=F28+G28			=SUM(I28:M28)						=IF(E28=H28,0,N27+E28-H28)
29	Total				=SUM(E9:E28)	=SUM(F9:F28)	=SUM(G9:G28)	=SUM(H9:H28)	=SUM(I9:I28)	=SUM	=SUN	=SUM	=SUM	=N8+E29-H29
30														

We could have added further features as follows, but we decided that, as this is petty cash, we had probably done enough! You may well have thought of these or others of your own.

(a)   Conditional functions to ensure that each line is used in turn.

(b)   Conditional function to cross check the contents of cell N29.

(c)   Linked worksheets to ensure that totals are automatically carried forward to the following week.

(d)   Formulae to calculate the amount to be banked or the cheque required to be cashed.

Answer to Activity 18

The completed spreadsheet is shown below. You should note the following.

(a)   We have treated the IOU as cash. Of course, writing IOUs should be discouraged from a control point of view.

(b)   We have formatted the spreadsheet to display figures to two decimal places.

(c)   The formula in cell G22 is =N8-N21. We could have set up separate columns for bank receipts and bank payments.

(d)   We formatted column B to display dates in DD-MMM format.

	A	B	C	D	E	F	G	H	I	J	K	L	M	N
1	Bright Ideas Ltd													
2	Petty cash				Week number:									
3					Week ending:									
4														
5														
6	Narrative	Date	Line	Ref	Receipts	Sales	Sundry	Payments	Postage	Stationery	Kitchen	Gifts	Sundry	Balance
7					£	£	£	£	£	£	£	£	£	£
8	Balance b/f													250.00
9	Cash sale	08-Sep	1	2388	25.60	25.60								275.60
10	Cash sale	08-Sep	2	2389	13.55	13.55								289.15
11	Coffee	08-Sep	3	4998				12.96			12.96			276.19
12	Cash sale	09-Sep	4	2390	25.60	25.60								301.79
13	Envelopes	09-Sep	5	4999				3.95		3.95				297.84
14	Stamps	09-Sep	6	4000				25.00	25.00					272.84
15	Cash sale	10-Sep	7	2391	4.00	4.00								276.84
16	Cash sale	10-Sep	8	2392	13.55	13.55								290.39
17	Wedding gift AF	10-Sep	9	4001				74.99				74.99		215.40
18	Taxi	11-Sep	10	4002				8.00					8.00	207.40
19	Cash sale	12-Sep	11	2393	12.00	12.00								219.40
20	Christian Aid	12-Sep	12	4003				20.00					20.00	199.40
21	Speedpost	12-Sep	13	4004				32.71	32.71					166.69
22	Cheque	12-Sep	14	Bank	83.31		83.31							250.00
23			15											
24			16											
25			17											
26			18											
27			19											
28			20											
29	Total				177.61	94.30	83.31	177.61	57.71	3.95	12.96	74.99	28.00	250.00

Answer to Activity 19

The completed job cost cards follow. There are many different ways of setting up this data: this is only one suggestion. Check the formulae we used in the file **Ac_19_S**

Note the following.

(a)   We have assumed that damaged stock cannot be identified with any particular job.

(b)   Actual overhead costs are irrelevant; it is the recovery percentages which are important here.

(c)   The spreadsheet has been designed to enable it to be used in other periods with other jobs.

(d)   An alternative would have been to use linked sheets (one sheet per month).

	A	B	C	D	E
1	**Bodger & Co**				
2	Summarised job cards				
3	September 20X5				
4					
5	*Costs b/f*				
6			*Job no. 487*		*Job no. 488*
7		Hours	£	Hours	£
8	Direct materials		1025.00		
9	Direct labour	120	525.00		
10	Production overhead		360.00		
11			1910.00		
12	*September*				
13	Direct materials		3585.00		5850.00
14	Material transfers		-1125.00		1125.00
15	Returns to stores		-1305.00		
16	Direct labour	445	2002.50	280	1260.00
17	Invoice value		8050.00		12000.00
18					
19	*Data table*	£			
20	Labour cost per hour	4.50			
21	Production o'head rate	3.00			
22	Admin/mkting o'head rate	0.2			
23					
24					
25	**Summarised job cost cards**				
26			*Job no. 487*		*Job no. 488*
27	Direct materials		2180.00		6975.00
28	Direct labour		2527.50		1260.00
29	Production overhead		1695.00		840.00
30	Factory cost		6402.50		9075.00
31	Admin/mkting o'head		1280.50		1815.00
32	Cost of sale		7683.00		10890.00
33	Invoice value		8050.00		12000.00
34	Profit/loss on job		367.00		1110.00
35					

Answer to Activity 20

The final ETB is shown below. You should have spotted that the 'bank' figure is an overdraft - otherwise your opening TB columns would not have balanced.

	A	B	C	D	E	F	G	H	I	J	K	L
1	Vincent											
2	ETB Year Ended 31/12/X7											
3	Account		Trial balance		Adjustments		Accrued	Prepaid	Profit and loss		Balance sheet	
4			£	£	£	£	£	£	£	£	£	£
5												
6	F & F cost	B	21,650								21,650	
7	F & F depn	B		(12,965)		(3,954)						(16,919)
8	MV cost	B	37,628								37,628	
9	MV depn	B		(17,490)		(8,643)						(26,133)
10	Stock at 01 Jan 20X7	P	34,285						34,285			
11	Sales ledger control	B	91,440		4,300	(2,440)					93,300	
12	Doubtful debt provision	B		(3,409)		(1,256)						(4,665)
13	Cash	B	361								361	
14	Bank	B		(14,297)								(14,297)
15	Purch ledger control	B		(102,157)								(102,157)
16	Sales	P		(354,291)		(4,300)				(358,591)		
17	Purchases	P	197,981						197,981			
18	Wages and salaries	P	57,980						57,980			
19	Rent and rates	P	31,650				6,750		38,400			
20	Advertising	P	12,240					(1,500)	10,740			
21	Administrative expenses	P	31,498						31,498			
22	Bank charges	P	2,133				508		2,641			
23	Bad debts written off	P	763		3,696				4,459			
24	Capital	B		(15,000)		(10,000)						(25,000)
25	Stock at 31 Dec 20X7	B			37,238						37,238	
26	Stock at 31 Dec 20X7	P				(37,238)				(37,238)		
27	Accruals	B					(7,258)					(7,258)
28	Prepayments	B						1,500			1,500	
29	Depreciation expense	P			12,597				12,597			
30	Sundry debtors	B			10,000						10,000	
31												
32												
33	SUB-TOTAL		519,609	(519,609)	67,831	(67,831)	8,758	(8,758)	390,581	(395,829)	201,677	(196,429)
34	Profit for the year								5,248			(5,248)
35	TOTAL		519,609	(519,609)	67,831	(67,831)	8,758	(8,758)	395,829	(395,829)	201,677	(201,677)

Adjustments and formulae used are shown on the next page. The adjustments regarding depreciation and the effect on the provision for bad debts of late sales required some careful thought.

	A	B	C	D	E
37					
38	**Adjustments**				
39	*Depreciation*				
40	MV		8643		
41	FF		3954		
42	Depreciation expense			12597	
43					
44	*Bad debts*				
45	Debtors		93,300		
46	Provision %		5%		
47	New provision		4665		
48	Current provision		-3,409		
49	Increase			1256	
50	Bad Debts		2440		
51				2440	
52				3696	
53					
54	*Stock*				
55	Closing stock		37238		
56					
57	**Accruals**				
58	Bank charges		508		
59	Rent		6750		
60				7258	
61					
62	**Prepayments**				
63					
64	Advertising		1500		
65				1500	
66					
67	**Sales**				
68	Post Xmas		4300		
69					
70	**Capital**				
71	New capital		10000		
72					

	A	B	C	D	E
37					
38	**Adjustments**				
39	*Depreciation*				
40	MV		=1146+((C8-7640)*0.25)		
41	FF		=(C6-1880)*0.2		
42	Depreciation expense			=SUM(C40:C41)	
43					
44	*Bad debts*				
45	Debtors		=(C11+C68)-2440		
46	Provision %		0.05		
47	New provision		=C46*C45		
48	Current provision		=D12		
49	Increase			=SUM(C47:C48)	
50	Bad Debts		2440		
51				=SUM(C49:C50)	
52				=SUM(D49:D51)	
53					
54	*Stock*				
55	Closing stock		37238		
56					
57	**Accruals**				
58	Bank charges		508		
59	Rent		6750		
60				=SUM(C58:C59)	
61					
62	**Prepayments**				
63					
64	Advertising		1500		
65				=SUM(C63:C64)	
66					
67	**Sales**				
68	Post Xmas		4300		
69					
70	**Capital**				
71	New capital		10000		
72					

Answer to Activity 21

The final spreadsheet is shown below and is available as **Ac_21_S** in the BPP data.

	A	B	C	D	E	F	G	H	I	J	K	L	M	N	O	P
1	Dittori Sage Ltd															
2	Debtors ageing by region															
3	Date - 31 May 20X6															
4																
5	Region	Balance	Current	1 month	2 month	3 month	4 month	5 month +		Curr	1mth	2mth	3 mth	4 mth	5 mth+	Total
6		£	£	£	£	£	£	£								
7	Highlands	1,001.41	346.60	567.84	32.17			54.80		34.6%	56.7%	3.2%			5.5%	100%
8	Strathclyde	59,578.78	24,512.05	28,235.50	4,592.50	1,244.80	51.36	942.57		41.1%	47.4%	7.7%	2.1%	0.1%	1.6%	100%
9	Borders	2,440.65	1,927.77		512.88					79.0%		21.0%				100%
10	North West	18,249.10	824.80	14,388.91	2,473.53		482.20	79.66		4.5%	78.8%	13.6%		2.6%	0.4%	100%
11	North East	32,243.59	14,377.20	12,850.00		3,771.84	1,244.55			44.6%	39.9%		11.7%	3.9%		100%
12	Midlands	140,737.86	45,388.27	61,337.88	24,001.02	4,288.31	1,391.27	4,331.11		32.3%	43.6%	17.1%	3.0%	1.0%	3.1%	100%
13	Wales	25,630.84	14,318.91	5,473.53	21.99	4,881.64	512.27	422.50		55.9%	21.4%	0.1%	19.0%	2.0%	1.6%	100%
14	East Anglia	3,242.14	157.20	943.68	377.40	1,500.87	15.33	247.66		4.8%	29.1%	11.6%	46.3%	0.5%	7.6%	100%
15	South West	32,735.50	9,528.73	11,983.39	3,771.89	6,228.77	1,008.21	214.51		29.1%	36.6%	11.5%	19.0%	3.1%	0.7%	100%
16	South East	225,179.78	68,110.78	83,914.54	29,117.96	24,285.10	14,328.90	5,422.50		30.2%	37.3%	12.9%	10.8%	6.4%	2.4%	100%
17	France	25,244.78	6,422.80	7,451.47	5,897.55	2,103.70	140.50	3,228.76		25.4%	29.5%	23.4%	8.3%	0.6%	12.8%	100%
18	Other EU	22,669.00	5,433.88	4,991.90	5,012.70	4,223.80	1,022.43	1,984.29		24.0%	22.0%	22.1%	18.6%	4.5%	8.8%	100%
19	Rest of world	10,121.21	1,822.70	4,529.67	277.50	3,491.34				18.0%	44.8%	2.7%	34.5%			100%
20	Total	599,074.64	193,171.69	236,668.31	76,089.09	56,020.17	20,197.02	16,928.36		32.2%	39.5%	12.7%	9.4%	3.4%	2.8%	100%

Formulae used are as follows (selected columns only: look at the file itself for the full formulae). Note the use of the absolute address in cell J7 to facilitate copying across and down. Column P is optional. Columns J to P can be formatted in % style.

	A	B	C	I	J	K	L	M	N	O	P
1	Dittori Sage Ltd										
2	Debtors ageing by region										
3	Date - 31 May 20X6										
4											
5	Region	Balance	Current		Curr	1mth	2 mth	3 mth	4 mth	5 mth+	Total
6		£	£								
7	Highlands	=SUM(C7:H7)	346.6		=C7/$B7	=D7/$B7	=E7/$B7	=F7/$B7	=G7/$B7	=H7/$B7	=SUM(J7:O7)
8	Strathclyde	=SUM(C8:H8)	24512.05		=C8/$B8	=D8/$B8	=E8/$B8	=F8/$B8	=G8/$B8	=H8/$B8	=SUM(J8:O8)
9	Borders	=SUM(C9:H9)	1927.77		=C9/$B9	=D9/$B9	=E9/$B9	=F9/$B9	=G9/$B9	=H9/$B9	=SUM(J9:O9)
10	North West	=SUM(C10:H10)	824.8		=C10/$B10	=D10/$B10	=E10/$B10	=F10/$B10	=G10/$B10	=H10/$B10	=SUM(J10:O10)
11	North East	=SUM(C11:H11)	14377.2		=C11/$B11	=D11/$B11	=E11/$B11	=F11/$B11	=G11/$B11	=H11/$B11	=SUM(J11:O11)
12	Midlands	=SUM(C12:H12)	45388.27		=C12/$B12	=D12/$B12	=E12/$B12	=F12/$B12	=G12/$B12	=H12/$B12	=SUM(J12:O12)
13	Wales	=SUM(C13:H13)	14318.91		=C13/$B13	=D13/$B13	=E13/$B13	=F13/$B13	=G13/$B13	=H13/$B13	=SUM(J13:O13)
14	East Anglia	=SUM(C14:H14)	157.2		=C14/$B14	=D14/$B14	=E14/$B14	=F14/$B14	=G14/$B14	=H14/$B14	=SUM(J14:O14)
15	South West	=SUM(C15:H15)	9528.73		=C15/$B15	=D15/$B15	=E15/$B15	=F15/$B15	=G15/$B15	=H15/$B15	=SUM(J15:O15)
16	South East	=SUM(C16:H16)	68110.78		=C16/$B16	=D16/$B16	=E16/$B16	=F16/$B16	=G16/$B16	=H16/$B16	=SUM(J16:O16)
17	France	=SUM(C17:H17)	6422.8		=C17/$B17	=D17/$B17	=E17/$B17	=F17/$B17	=G17/$B17	=H17/$B17	=SUM(J17:O17)
18	Other EU	=SUM(C18:H18)	5433.88		=C18/$B18	=D18/$B18	=E18/$B18	=F18/$B18	=G18/$B18	=H18/$B18	=SUM(J18:O18)
19	Rest of world	=SUM(C19:H19)	1822.7		=C19/$B19	=D19/$B19	=E19/$B19	=F19/$B19	=G19/$B19	=H19/$B19	=SUM(J19:O19)
20	Total	=SUM(B7:B19)	=SUM(C7:C19)		=C20/$B20	=D20/$B20	=E20/$B20	=F20/$B20	=G20/$B20	=H20/$B20	=SUM(J20:O20)

PROFESSIONAL EDUCATION

Answer to Activity 22

NPV at 10%	£12,030	The project should be accepted because it gives a positive NPV	
NPV at 11%	-£48,815	The project should be rejected because it gives a negative NPV	

As the NPV at 10% is positive, and the NPV at 11% is negative, the IRR must be between 10% and 11%. As shown below, it is 10.19%.

The spreadsheet used to calculate these figures is shown below. You can have a closer look by opening the file **Ac_22_S** in the BPP data.

	A	B	C	D	E	F
1	**NPV calculation**				**IRR calculation**	
2						
3	Costs incurred now		-1,500,000		Costs incurred now	-1,500,000
4	Savings year 1	271,000			Savings year 1	271,000
5	Savings year 2	226,000			Savings year 2	226,000
6	Savings year 3	249,000			Savings year 3	249,000
7	Savings year 4	275,000			Savings year 4	275,000
8	Savings year 5	265,000			Savings year 5	265,000
9	Savings year 6	300,000			Savings year 6	300,000
10	Savings year 7	177,000			Savings year 7	177,000
11	Savings year 8	205,000			Savings year 8	205,000
12	Savings year 9	223,000			Savings year 9	223,000
13	Savings year 10	231,000			Savings year 10	231,000
14	Discounted value		1,512,030			
15	**Net present value**		12,030		**IRR**	10.19%
16						
17						
18						
19	**Rate**	10%				

The formulae are shown below.

	A	B	C	D	E	F
1	**NPV calculation**				**IRR calculation**	
2						
3	Costs incurred now		-1500000		Costs incurred now	-1500000
4	Savings year 1	271000			Savings year 1	271000
5	Savings year 2	226000			Savings year 2	226000
6	Savings year 3	249000			Savings year 3	249000
7	Savings year 4	275000			Savings year 4	275000
8	Savings year 5	265000			Savings year 5	265000
9	Savings year 6	300000			Savings year 6	300000
10	Savings year 7	177000			Savings year 7	177000
11	Savings year 8	205000			Savings year 8	205000
12	Savings year 9	223000			Savings year 9	223000
13	Savings year 10	231000			Savings year 10	231000
14	Discounted value		=NPV(B19,B4:B13)			
15	**Net present value**		=SUM(C3:C14)		**IRR**	=IRR(F3:F13)
16						
17						
18						
19	**Rate**	0.1				

Answer to Activity 23

A standard data **Sort** is not useful as the data consists of a mixture of letters and numbers within each cell. We need to start by separating the alphabetical data from numerical data.

There is a useful function in Excel that allows you to do this.

In the solution shown below the formula in column B **=RIGHT(A1,2)** extracts the two rightmost characters from the entry in column A, while the formula in column C **=LEFT(A1,4)** extracts the four leftmost characters.

The data can then be sorted – using column B as the main sort criteria and column C as the secondary criteria. The first 25 rows of the results are shown below.

	A	B	C
1	4842AA	AA	4842
2	5736AA	AA	5736
3	8162AA	AA	8162
4	7635AB	AB	7635
5	7880AB	AB	7880
6	8884AB	AB	8884
7	6856AC	AC	6856
8	6851AD	AD	6851
9	3320AE	AE	3320
10	3635AE	AE	3635
11	5571AF	AF	5571
12	8406AF	AF	8406
13	6139AG	AG	6139
14	6305AG	AG	6305
15	8282AG	AG	8282
16	1118AI	AI	1118
17	9581AI	AI	9581
18	7540AJ	AJ	7540
19	7733AJ	AJ	7733
20	3679AK	AK	3679
21	9337AK	AK	9337
22	5929AL	AL	5929
23	6171AL	AL	6171
24	6248AL	AL	6248
25	8507AL	AL	8507

The full answer is provided in the BPP file **Ac_23_S**

The question of duplicates is dealt with in columns D and E of our answer. Once you have sorted the data you can do a simple test to see if the entry in one row equal to the entry in the previous row, and return 1 if so, 0 if not: **=IF(A2=A1,1,0)**. You then sum the column in which your 1's and 0s are returned. This saves you having to look right through 1500 records. If it sums to more than 0, you know there is a duplicate entry.

To find it quickly, copy the column with the duplicate-finding formulae into the next column as a **number** (in Excel, **Edit ... Paste Special ... Values)** and then do a computer search (**Edit Find)** just on row E, for the number 1.

You should have found one duplicate: the item coded **1005FL** appears twice.

Answer to Activity 24

The file **Ac_24_S** shows you how this is done. Use your spreadsheet experience to explore the spreadsheet yourself and establish how it has been constructed. (Tick the box found in Tools, Options, Formulas (in the View Tab) to view the formulae.)

PART C

Assignments

Assignments are designed to enable you to apply your Excel skills in realistic situations.

		Assignment	Answer to assignment	Done
1	Broom Riggs	79	103	
2	Wild Thyme	83	103	
3	Island Quay	85	103	
4	Marvels Ltd	91	104	
5	Harry Alexander Ltd	95	112	
6	KoolFoot	99	118	

Assignment 1:
Broom Riggs

Information

Broom Riggs Ltd is a company engaged in the sale of watersports equipment and accessories. It was established in 20X1 and operates from leasehold retail premises. Although its customer base consists mainly of individual callers, it does also supply some goods to trade customers, for example, a local water-ski club and two sailing clubs.

The company is now preparing accounts for the year ended 31 December 20X8. The trial balance as at 31 December 20X8 is as follows. This is available in the file **ASS1_BROOM_Q** in the BPP data.

Folio	Account	DR £	CR £
A1	Accountancy fees	440.00	
A2	Advertising	1,556.29	
B1	Bank account		27,488.12
B2	Bank charges	2,157.51	
B3	Bank interest	1,109.11	
B4	Bad debt expense		
C1	Credit card charges	2,212.80	
D1	Discounts allowed	5,629.31	
D2	Discounts received		4,529.69
D3	Directors' loan accounts	9,343.89	
D4	Depreciation (accumulated)		
	Fixtures and fittings		14,304.00
	Motor vehicles		22,563.10
	Leasehold		38,500.00
D5	Depreciation expense		
D6	Doubtful debt provision		
E1	Electricity	7,264.61	
F1	Fixtures and fittings	35,430.00	
G1	Gas	12,374.97	
I1	Insurance	22,298.96	
L1	Leasehold	220,000.00	
L2	Loan		50,000.00
L3	Loan interest	5,000.00	
M1	Maintenance	4,649.22	
M2	Motor expenses	1,557.10	
M3	Motor vehicles	73,482.10	

Folio	Account	DR	CR
P1	Profit and loss account		160,808.95
P2	Purchases	499,227.91	
P3	Purchase ledger control account		51,444.74
P4	Petty cash	1,000.00	
P5	Purchase returns		687.08
P6	Print, post and stationery	5,885.32	
P7	PAYE and NI	91,799.27	
R1	Rates	30,616.08	
R2	Rent (warehouse)	18,125.00	
S1	Share capital		100,000.00
S2	Sales		1,022,734.87
S3	Sales ledger control account	105,947.07	
S4	Sales returns	2,287.03	
S5	Staff welfare	1,768.56	
S6	Stock at 1 January 20X8	48,172.29	
S7	Sundry expenses	1,574.68	
T1	Telephone	8,763.82	
V1	VAT		18,965.89
W1	Wages and salaries	266,449.27	
W2	Water rates	9,454.27	
X1	Suspense account	16,450.00	

The following transactions and adjustments must be taken into account in the preparation of the trial balance.

(a) Fixed asset adjustments required are as follows.

    (i) The lease, which has a 40 year term, was purchased on 1 January 20X1. Depreciation, which is to be calculated on a straight line basis, has not yet been provided for the year ended 31 December 20X8.

    (ii) Depreciation has not yet been provided on the motor vehicles, which are depreciated at 25% on written down value.

    (iii) Depreciation is also still to be provided on fixtures and fittings at 10% of cost. A full year of depreciation is charged in the year of acquisition.

(b) The suspense account comprises the following items.

    (i) A new piece of fixed asset furniture was purchased during the year for £12,250.00 for cash but it was posted to the suspense account as it had not been classified.

    (ii) The company had paid £4,000 in cash for maintenance work but the bookkeeper had been unsure about whether to treat it as a capital or revenue item and it had been posted to the suspense account. The entire amount relates to revenue expenditure.

    (iii) The cash paid near the year end for the staff Christmas party (£450.00) had been posted to the suspense account

(iv)   One of the directors put an expenses claim in for £250.00 at the end of the year and this has been posted to the suspense account rather than the director's loan account. The relevant expense accounts have already been adjusted.

(c)   Bank charges to be posted are as follows.

    (i)   A bank statement received at the end of January showed that bank charges of £522.18 had been incurred for the three months ended 31 January 20X9.

    (ii)   The last time bank interest was charged was 31 October 20X8. The average overdrawn balance in November and December was £22,000. The prevailing average interest rate was 12% per annum.

(d)   Stock related items are as follows.

    (i)   On 2 January 20X9, goods with a cost of £511.42, which had been purchased by the company before the year end on credit, were returned to suppliers. The goods had been omitted from the year-end stock valuation.

    (ii)   Goods sold for £2,117.28 were returned by customers just after the year end. The stock has been included in the year end stock figure at cost, but no other adjustment has been made.

    (iii)   The closing stock was counted and valued at £67,329.53.

(e)   It has been discovered after the year end that a trade debtor owing £2,200.00 has gone into liquidation and there is no prospect of recovering any of the money. It has also been decided that, for the first time, a general provision should be made for doubtful debts. This is to be calculated as ½% of net trade debtors.

(f)   Other matters are as follows.

    (i)   An insurance bill was paid on 1 April 20X8 for £18,178.44 for the year to 31 March 20X9

    (ii)   The audit fee of £3,000.00 must be accrued under accountancy fees.

    (iii)   On 29 December 20X8 the company paid £3,625.00 rent for the quarter to 25 March 20X9.

    (iv)   The Uniform Business Rate paid on 1 April 20X8 for 12 months was £24,492.88

    (v)   The water rates bill paid on 1 April 20X8 for 12 months was £7,954.28.

Tasks

(a)   Set up a spreadsheet which will be used to prepare an extended trial balance. Enter the opening trial balance as at 31 December 20X8 and ensure that it balances. Save it on the computer's hard disk.

(b)   Print out the opening trial balance including the folio references, account names, debits and credits.

(c)   Obtain a floppy disk and check that it is free from viruses.

(d)   Create a folder called BROOM on this floppy disk and save the trial balance in this folder.

(e)   Delete your trial balance from the hard disk, and, once you have closed down the spreadsheet application and any other open applications, switch off your computer and any related peripheral devices.

(f)   Switch the computer back on and *copy* your spreadsheet file back onto the hard disk.

(g)   Set the floppy disk to write protect.

(h)   Returning to your spreadsheet, make the adjustments required to the trial balance and complete the extended trial balance. Document any calculations you make either on paper or on the spreadsheet, and submit these with your work.

(i)   Save the completed ETB (as, say, BROOM1) on the floppy disk you used earlier. Do *not* overwrite any files already on the floppy disk.

(j)   Print out on a single sheet of paper the complete spreadsheet containing the ETB.

Assignment 2: Wild Thyme

Information

Wild Thyme Ltd is a company which makes tents. It has three production departments and two service departments.

The cutting and sewing department (C) occupies 3,000 square metres of floor space, the frame-making department (F) 1,750 square metres and the assembly operation (A), which deals with such matters as stitching on of zips and guy ropes, 1,500 square metres.

The maintenance department (M) occupies 800 square metres and the staff restaurant (R) occupies 600 square metres.

Budgeted rent and rates costs for 20X7 are £8.20 per square metre for the whole of the site.

Other details relating to these departments are set out below. All figures are budgeted for the coming year, 20X7. These details are not available on file.

Departmental statistics	C	F	A	M	R
Plant value (£'000)	32	20	16	8	4
Hourly labour rate	£4.10	£5.14	£4.25	£4.00	£3.20
Direct labour hours	4,200	1,200	2,000		

Allocated overheads	C	F	A	M	R
Specific to each department (£'000)	4.8	2.2	3.5	2.0	1.6
Maintenance	20%	58%	22%		
Restaurant	55%	18%	27%		

Rent and rates costs are to be apportioned on the basis of floor area.

Other budgeted costs, and the relevant basis of apportionment for each, are set out below

Overhead	Total £	Basis of apportionment
Machine insurance	8,350	Plant value
Depreciation	16,450	Plant value
Production supervisor	24,300	Direct labour hours
Heat and light	8,800	Floor area

Tasks

(a)   Prepare a spreadsheet showing the overhead cost budgeted for each department.

(b)   You are told that the figures on this spreadsheet are confidential. How could you ensure only those people authorised to see the figures are able to open the spreadsheet file - assuming it was saved on an area of the computer network accessible by all?

(c)   Using the data provided, calculate overhead absorption rates for each department based on direct labour hours.

(d)   Improve the presentation of your spreadsheet (including the data table prepared in part (a)) so that it is suitable for inclusion in a management report.

(e)   Print out a copy of the final spreadsheet on a single sheet of paper.

(f)   You learn that the budget, which has now been agreed, includes two amendments. The production supervisor's costs will be £25,200 and heat and light are expected to cost £9,500. Revise your spreadsheet accordingly.

(g)   Close down all open applications and switch off your equipment.

Assignment 3: Island Quay

Information

Your company, Island Quay plc, is in the process of setting up a Customer Services department. Your supervisor is the Chief Accountant. She is keen to set up an accurate system of performance reporting for the department.

The department will not, in the short term at least, generate any income of its own. The Board wishes to monitor the departments performance carefully, following an initial investment of £180,000.

The department receives sales data from the sales order processing department and, acting on this, processes and issues warranty documentation whenever a warranty sale is made. A record is kept of the number of warranties issued as a measure of output. When a customer requires a warranty repair (following initial investigation by telephone), he or she completes a warranty claim form included in the documentation and posts or faxes it to the department setting out details of the problem or breakdown encountered.

When a warranty claim is received (on average one year into the life of the warranty), a repair is carried out. The number of repairs is also seen as a measure of output.

The department will also have responsibility for carrying out a component testing programme and for performing a limited amount of additional research.

Resources used by the department comprise labour, other running costs (including cost of spare parts and consumables) and the cost of capital.

The department is expected initially to use resources on the following activities, in the proportions shown below.

Issuing warranties	5%
Warranty repairs	60%
Testing	25%
Research	10%

Tasks

Your supervisor has devised a format for performance reporting. She has left you a set of notes, and has left the office for a week's management training course. She expects your work to be completed before her return.

(a)   Design a spreadsheet which could be used to report the required variables over a four year period. Include suitable sub-headings rather than simply listing all the variables in one group.

(b)   Insert the relevant data from your supervisor's notes and complete the spreadsheet. You will need to refer to your own notes of telephone calls as well in order to complete this task.

(c)   Save the spreadsheet and close down all applications.

(d)   Print out a copy of the final spreadsheet on a single sheet of paper. Use appropriate formatting functions to improve its appearance.

Inter-office memo

To: Accounting Technician
From: Chief Accountant

Can you have the performance report ready for me to take into the divisional board meeting on my return? We need to include the following items.

1   *Inflation.* Use Year 1 as a base, then allow for inflation as follows.

Year 1:	1.00
Year 2:	1.04
Year 3:	1.08
Year 4:	1.13
Year 5:	1.19

2   *Value of capital.* We need to depreciate the department's capital over five years, on a straight line basis, and adjust the depreciated value for inflation. (Eg, value of capital in year 2 is £180,000 × 0.8 × 1.04 and in year 3 it is £180,000 × 0.6 × 1.08.)

3   *Annual capital charge.* This is the amount of depreciation (inflated) plus an allowance for the cost of capital, calculated as 7% of the mid-year value. So in year one the charge is £47,542. (This is calculated as

$$£180,000 \times 0.2 + \frac{£180,000 + £149,760}{2} \times 7\% \;.)$$

4   *'Physical' capital consumed.* Annual capital charge deflated by general price deflator.

5   *Hours worked.* Check with customer services director.

6   *Labour costs.* £205,000 in year 1, £200,000 in year 2 and rising by 2% in each subsequent year.

7   *Average wage rate.* This must be shown.

8   *Other running costs.* Check with finance director.

9   *'Physical' other running costs.* This is other running costs deflated.

10   *Total annual cost.* Put in a total which adds annual capital charge (3), labour costs (6) and other running costs (8).

11   *Total "physical" running costs.* Add 'physical' other running costs and physical labour (obtained from hours worked weighted by the base year unit cost, ie hours worked multiplied by the Year 1 average wage rate).

12   *Total 'physical' resources consumed.* This is total 'physical' running costs and 'physical' capital consumed.

13   *Warranties issued.* Check with customer services manager.

14   *Repairs performed.* Check with customer services manager.

15   *Total costs: issuing warranties.* Take relevant percentage of total annual cost.

16   *Unit cost: issuing warranties.* Must be shown.

17   *Real unit cost of issuing warranties.* Divide unit cost by general price deflator

18   *Total costs: performing repairs.* See (15).

19   *Unit cost: performing repairs.* As above. Assume £250 in Year 1. Remember that repairs are a year later than warranty issues, so take previous year cost from (18), inflate by cost of capital and by general price deflator relative to the previous year, then divide by current year output.

20   *Real unit cost of performing repairs.* As for warranties (see above).

21   *'Physical' output of warranties and repairs.* This is the sum of the outputs weighted by their respective base year (Year 1) unit costs, so in Year 1 we take 6400 × unit cost of issuing warranty + 620 × £250.

22   *'Physical' running costs: warranties and repairs.* Take relevant percentage of Total 'physical' running costs.

23   *Productivity of running costs: warranties and repairs.* This is calculated from the previous two lines and is obtained by dividing 'physical' output by 'physical' running costs.

24   *Year-on-year increase in (23).* Put this in as a percentage.

25   *Total ''physical' resources consumed: warranties and repairs.* Calculated on same basis as (22).

26   *Productivity of all resources: warranties and repairs.* Divide previous line into 'physical' output of warranties and repairs.

27   *Year-on-year increase in (26).* Show as percentage.

Note of telephone call.

Customer services director.

Hours worked in department: 30,000 per annum.

Note of telephone call.

Finance director's PA

Other running costs are as follows:

£62,000 in year 1, then £2,000 increase in each of next 2 years and £64,000 in year 4.

Note of telephone call.

Customer Services Manager

Year	Warranties	Repairs
1	6,400	620
2	6,800	700
3	6,800	640
4	7,000	660

Assignment 4:
Marvels Ltd

Information

The situation

Introduction

Marvels Ltd is a manufacturing company which has been operating for just over a year. The company makes small but ingenious gadgets for the DIY market, invented by Charles Davis, who is the Managing Director of the company. Business was slow to begin with, but sales have rocketed since one of the company's products was featured in a popular television programme on home improvements.

Marvels Ltd now has over 400 customers including major DIY stores in many of the larger cities in the UK (the company is based in London). Repeat orders are regular because the gadget lasts for about three months before it is worn out and has to be replaced.

At present the company's success is making it difficult to meet demand, and it has grown so quickly that administrative matters have been neglected. Expansion plans are under way, including new premises and a number of new staff, of which you, a qualified accountant, are the first to be appointed.

The accounting records

In the opening months of business records were kept using a manual system. These records have gradually been transferred onto spreadsheets representing the major areas of the business (purchases, sales, cash etc). However, the system has become difficult to maintain and there are frequently discrepancies between one set of figures and another.

The sales ledger, for instance, shows name, address and telephone number information, and analyses debts outstanding by age. Debts older than 90 days are written off. There have been very few write-offs to date.

Here are selected rows and columns from the spreadsheet to give you an idea of what you will find (note, some columns are hidden in this illustration for reasons of space).

	A	B	E	F	K	L	M
1					31-60	61-90	Total
2	Fads	Putney High Street	London	SW15 1SP	246.97	62.62	577.15
3	B & Q DIY Supercentre	Blythwood Industrial Estate	Renfrew	PA4 9EU	1087.00	168.24	2885.75
4	D I Y Woodstock	111 A Neilston Road	Paisley	PA2 6ER	524.37	15.92	1326.85
5	D T S	Chester Road East	Deeside	CH5 1QD	537.66	66.60	1261.40
6	Tuck & Norris Ltd	622 Lordship Lane	London	N22 5JH	756.18	72.50	1332.80
7	Cardiff Paint Supplies	51-53 Carlisle Street	Cardiff	CF2 2DR	641.98	117.27	1243.55
8	Great Mills D I Y	Beardmore Park	Ipswich	IP5 7RX	688.37	12.08	1219.75
9	Do-it-yourself	82 Niddrie Road	Glasgow	G42 8PU	257.29	68.51	583.10
10	Homecare Electrics	6 Arndale Square	Newcastle Upon Tyne	NE12 8SE	504.14	76.19	1172.15
11	Do It Yourself Supplies	84 Church Road	Bristol	BS5 9JY	1550.82	69.12	2742.95
12	Mercury Stores Hdwre Shop	43 Chalcot Road	London	NW1 8LS	607.00	29.89	1094.80
13	Newmans	31 Cherry Tree Avenue	Dover	CT16 2NL	889.70	54.11	1701.70
14	Bob Leach D I Y & Timber Store	101 Botley Road	Southampton	SO52 9DT	1023.08	245.22	2570.40
15	S D I Y Bill Centre	8 Undercliff Road West	Felixstowe	IP11 8AW	929.78	18.39	1915.90
16	DIY Supplies	17 St James Street	Okehampton	EX20 1DJ	1315.23	233.23	2540.65
17	Pretty Chic	Greenhole Place	Aberdeen	AB23 8EU	300.68	5.18	523.60
18	Manor Utilities Hire Contractors	41 Bridge Road	Southampton	SO2 7DT	357.66	19.79	749.70
19	Fads The Decorating Specialists	Glasgow (Easterhouse)	Glasgow	G34 9DT	261.37	8.39	630.70
20	Murray Timber Supplies Timber & DIY	3 The Mans	London	NW6 1NY	44.83	0.36	107.10
21	Scotts Hardware D I Y Shop	4 Ellenbrook Green	Ipswich	IP2 9RR	233.41	29.45	446.25
22	Exmouth Handyman	15 Exeter Road	Exmouth	EX8 1PN	820.69	54.67	1469.65
23	G Fox & Sons	139 Clouds Hill Road	Bristol	BS5 7LH	1155.42	248.10	2606.10
24	Do-it-yourself Supplies	35/37 New Street	Carnforth	LA5 9BX	330.56	24.20	672.35
25	Great Mills D I Y Superstore	Rannoch Road	Glasgow	G71 5PR	950.56	204.35	2522.80
26	Sullivans Home Improvement Centre	334 Gloucester Road	Bristol	BS7 8TJ	23.06	3.25	59.50
27	Fads	124 Rye Lane	London	SE15 4RZ	254.75	17.17	464.10
28	Homebase Ltd	Fox Den Road	Bristol	BS12 6SS	984.67	2.16	2403.80
29	Rkp Hardware	51 Englands Lane	London	NW3 4YD	1095.85	5.17	2150.00
30	Walparite	26 Bell Street	Romsey	SO51 8GW	1499.23	59.17	2689.40
31	R Hammersley	44 High Street	Mold	CH7 1BH	76.42	27.80	214.20
32	A G Stanley Ltd	224 Walworth Road	London	SE17 1JE	1011.40	48.16	2112.25
33	Wasons Paint Paper & D I Y Centre	Office	Penarth	CF6 1JD	405.41	26.56	737.80
34	Do It All Limited	Wrexham	Wrexham	LL13 8DH	730.76	19.95	1511.30
35	Sullivans Home Improvement Centre	10 Arnside Road	Bristol	BS10 6AT	732.27	45.24	1570.80
36	D I Y Whitchurch	20 Bell Street	Whitchurch	RG28 7AE	902.22	147.15	1951.60
37	Golders Green D I Y	5 Russell Parade	London	NW11 9NN	165.36	36.98	440.30
38	Timber & Tools	776 Stockport Road	Manchester	M12 4GD	661.73	18.59	1291.15
39	Spectrum Home & Garden Centre	Mold Road	Wrexham	LL12 9UR	894.74	24.88	1594.60
40	Treasure Finder Ii	Westhill Shopping Centre	Skene	AB32 6RL	894.28	0.00	1987.30
41	Ace Decore Colour & Design Centre	Unit 8 Clarence Street	Chorley	PR7 2AT	1025.06	206.85	2070.60

It has been decided that Marvels requires an accounting software package. Existing accounting records need to be transferred to this new system as soon as possible. You will play an important part in this task.

Your Role

You have decided that tackling the sales ledger records is your first priority. Besides tidying up the ledgers and eliminating errors and inconsistencies as far as possible you wish to identify and analyse trends that may be helpful to management, for instance to focus their marketing efforts in the right areas, and to improve cash flow.

Tasks

1. Load the spreadsheet filename **ASS4_MARVELS_Q,** save it with a name of your own choosing, and improve its general appearance and readability by adding titles, sheet names and formatting as you see fit. **Do not make any changes to the data at this stage**.

2. Devise a coding system and allocate a code number to each customer.

   The names of some customers have been entered inconsistently. For instance Texas are called "Texas Homecare", "Texas Homecare Home Improvements", "Texas Homecare Ltd", and so on. Identify and edit out such inconsistencies in your copy of the spreadsheet. If you are not sure that two customers should have the same name, leave both names as they are but make a note of them for further enquiry.

   There are also **four** clear duplicate entries that you must find and **four** possible duplicates. Write a memo to Sami Johnswell, the customer services supervisor, giving him details of the sixteen accounts concerned, so that he can investigate whether the customers concerned are happy for the debts due to be amalgamated.

3. Mr Davis has asked you for some information about geographical sales patterns. Analyse the appropriate data in the spreadsheet and prepare a brief report for Mr Davis providing him with whatever information you think might be useful.

   Make a note of any further discrepancies you find during this exercise, such as missing information, or unusual or erroneous entries.

4. Mr Davis is also concerned about the company's overdraft and would like some information about debtors and cash collection.

   Before you begin make a new copy of your spreadsheet and correct the discrepancies you found in Task 3.

   Then verify that the Total column correctly sums the aged balances. Make a note of any discrepancies. When you have done this assume that the addition has been done incorrectly and recreate the total column using a formula.

   You can then analyse the information and summarise your findings in a report to Mr Davis, together with any comments that you feel should be made.

5. Mr Davis has asked Ranju, one of his sales staff, to chase up significant outstanding amounts.

   On a separate sheet prepare a list of debtors with amounts of over £1,500 outstanding for more than 30 days. Include any information that may be useful for Ranju, and any extra columns that may help her in her administration of this task.

Assignment 5:
Harry Alexander Ltd

Information

The situation

Harry Alexander Ltd is a company that carries out restoration work on vintage motor vehicles. The company has between seven and fifteen vehicles being restored on its premises per month.

The company usually charges a single price of £10,000 for a restoration, irrespective of the actual costs incurred, although if a job is clearly going to be particularly difficult the customer is asked to agree to reimburse the company for its costs plus a mark-up on cost of a third.

The work involves quite a considerable amount of labour by skilled mechanics and their assistants and trainees, and also the replacement of a large number of components.

The company has a number of stand-alone Pentium PCs which are used for administrative purposes in the sales, marketing and personnel departments, and to maintain financial accounting records. Costing is done using spreadsheets.

The accounting records

Materials issued from stores are given consecutive issue note numbers of five digits. The issue note records the Job number, the materials code and the quantity issued. Issue notes are pre-numbered and pre-printed with the relevant headings. They are completed manually by stores staff.

Employees are required to record the hours they spend on each job on a job card, which they fill in by hand, usually at the end of each day. Jobs are then costed for materials and labour by entering data from the issue notes and job cards onto a spreadsheet and applying the relevant costs to each item.

Just before she left the company, your predecessor entered all the issue note information and employee hours for October 20X4 into a spreadsheet. An extract, showing how the spreadsheet looks at present follows.

	A	B	C	D	E	F	G	H	I
1	Issue note	Job	Materials code	Quantity	Materials Cost	Employee	Job	Labour hours	Labour cost
2	47023	728	AH8317	35		P002	726	77	
3	47024	732	TP7325	29		P002	728	67	
4	47025	733	ED2677	51		P002	732	40	
5	47026	731	QE2207	62		P003	726	24	
6	47027	731	YR8218	61		P003	728	40	
7	47028	724	ED2677	57		P003	731	37	
8	47029	724	PF6023	50		P003	733	83	
9	47030	726	XC5229	13		P004	724	42	
10	47031	732	WL5592	13		P004	727	77	
11	47032	729	RK3583	54		P004	731	31	
12	47033	729	ZB2520	1		P004	732	34	
13	47034	728	QE2207	45		P005	724	68	
14	47035	730	YR8218	15		P005	727	61	
15	47036	726	GY2898	6		P005	728	55	
16	47037	729	UQ7049	21		P006	724	34	
17	47038	729	CZ8997	30		P006	726	29	
18	47039	729	DN9569	32		P006	731	79	
19	47040	729	PF6023	53		P006	732	42	

Materials have codes consisting of two letters followed by 4 numbers. For the month of October 20X4 the following costs apply.

Material	£
KM6315	8.45
ED2677	8.03
NG7732	6.93
DN9569	6.59
BX3662	5.94
QE2207	5.67
CZ8997	5.38
JV7549	4.35
HU2871	4.00
RK3583	3.60
YR8218	3.44
WL5592	3.29
PF6023	2.81
TP7325	2.34
ZB2520	2.04
VA1662	1.84
UQ7049	1.68
MT9908	1.14
AH8317	1.01
FW4100	0.70
LJ1234	0.66
XC5229	0.59
GY2898	0.27

Employees are given an employee number in the form P001, P002 and so on. Employees are paid at the following hourly rates.

Employee	£
P001	15.00
P002	12.00
P003	12.00
P004	12.00
P005	12.00
P006	12.00
P007	12.00
P008	9.60
P009	9.60
P010	9.60
P011	9.60
P012	7.70
P013	7.70
P014	7.70
P015	7.70
P016	7.70
P017	7.70
P018	7.70
P019	7.70
P020	7.70
P021	7.70
P022	4.80
P023	4.80
P024	3.60

Your Role

You have just been appointed as a cost accountant at Harry Alexander Ltd. The Production Manager has asked you to complete the cost analysis spreadsheet and to provide a variety of information which will be used for determining profitability and to maintain control over the organisation.

The tasks are set out in the next section and you should carry these out in such a way that you can hand over to the Production Manager a package of material (modified spreadsheets, notes, reports and so on) that he can work on over the next few days.

Tasks

1. Open the spreadsheet **ASS5_HARRY_Q** from the files provided with this book. Save the spreadsheet with a name of your own choosing. On a separate part of the sheet, or on another sheet, enter the data for materials costs and employee costs (as provided in the Assignment information).

2. Making appropriate use of formulae, complete the columns for Materials Cost and Labour Cost. Using the spreadsheet, work out the total materials cost, the total labour cost, and the total cost of materials and labour together.

3. Prepare a report for the Production Manager which includes information on the cost of each job. Make comments, and include a chart or charts, as you feel appropriate, for instance identifying highest and lowest cost, average cost, and so on.

   When you have written your report make notes and queries for your own use about what other information you would like to have so that you can produce more meaningful analyses in the future. These might include comments about the data and/or comments about the nature of the business and the way it is run in general.

4. The Production Manager has asked for some information on the use of materials. In particular he has asked you to have a look at Job 730, which was an almost identical job to Job 718, completed in September 20X4, and at material TP7325, of which 520 units were used in September and which he says he would expect to be used in practically equal quantities on every job.

   Here are the details of materials usage for Job 718.

Material	Quantity	Material	Quantity
AH8317	7	MT9908	40
BX3662	36	NG7732	60
CZ8997	40	PF6023	124
DN9569	22	QE2207	10
ED2677	80	RK3583	50
FW4100	42	UQ7049	80
HU2871	5	WL5592	34
JV7549	62	YR8218	47
KM6315	70	ZB2520	149
LJ1234	75		

   Prepare a report which provides some useful information on the matter of Job 730 and on the use of material TP7325.

5. The Production Manager also monitors the time taken on each job. Prepare a brief note showing which jobs took the longest and shortest times, the average time for each job, and which employee took the longest amount of time on which job.

Assignment 6: KoolFoot

Information

The situation

When Jane Jones inherited the family shoe shop in November 20X3, she made some dramatic changes. She could see that the business was no longer able to compete with the national chains and so reorganised the business completely. She got rid of the traditional wide range of shoes of all styles and, for all age groups, replaced them with a range of training shoes. She redesigned the shop and changed the name to KoolFoot. She decided to specialise in a limited range of high-quality trainers from four of the major manufacturers with a strategy of buying in bulk to keep down the costs of purchases and passing on the savings to her customers. The objective is to achieve a high volume of sales to strengthen her negotiating position with her suppliers.

The business is currently a small one, operating from a shop of 150 square metres in a small market town. Jane hopes to prove that her business ideas are sound and then to expand into neighbouring towns as soon as possible. She employs two full time assistants and manages the shop herself. From her observations and from the cash-flow generated in the first full year of trading in the new manner, she is convinced that she will succeed.

It is now the end of March 20X5 and KoolFoot is at the end of the first full year's trading. Jane is getting ready to send her financial records to her accountant for accounts to be prepared. She knows that you are training to be an accounting technician and have some knowledge about how to use information technology and has asked you to help with getting some of the information together with regard to sales and stock levels.

The stock and stock records

The shop specialises in the following brands of trainers.

- Hike
- Oddidos
- Panther
- NY Gear

The shop offers nine styles from each manufacturer.

KoolFoot uses the European shoe sizes, and each size is stocked for boys and girls and alternate sizes for men and women. The sizes stocked are shown in the following table.

Boys-size		Girls-size	
	26		26
	27		27
	28		28
	29		29
	30		30
	31		31
	32		32
	33	Womens-size	34
	34		36
	35		38
	36		40
	37		42
Mens-size	38		44
	40		
	42		
	44		
	46		
	48		

Jane has kept stock records on a spreadsheet. This spreadsheet is available within the BPP data under the file name **ASS6_KOOL_Q**

The spreadsheet is based on a simple coding system that indicates the important details of the stock and shows the position at 28 March 2001.

The first character of the code indicates the brand: **H** for Hike, **O** for Oddidos, **P** for Panther and **N** for NY Gear.

The next character (1 to 9) indicates the **style**, the next character is a **B**, **M**, **G** or **W** for boy, man, girl or woman and the final character in the code indicates the shoe **size**.

For example, the code H2W34 indicates a Hike shoe, in style 2, a woman's shoe and size 34. N8B36 means a NY Gear shoe, in style 8, for a boy and size 36.

Jane has updated her stock every week and has consolidated the data on to the **ASS6_KOOL_Q** spreadsheet. An extract follows.

Count	Product Code	Opening stock	Sales	Deliveries
1	H1B26	1	0	1
2	H1B27	1	1	1
3	H1B28	1	1	1
4	H1B29	2	2	2
5	H1B30	0	2	2
6	H1B31	2	1	1
7	H1B32	0	1	1
8	H1B33	1	2	2
9	H1B34	0	1	1
10	H1B35	2	3	3
11	H1B36	0	2	2
12	H1B37	1	2	3
13	H1M38	0	5	5

Your Role

Jane is very busy with the day to day management of the shop and has asked you to carry out some analysis of her figures to assist her in providing year end information for her accountant and to give her a better insight into the way the business is working. The tasks are set out in the next section and you should carry these out in such a way that you can hand over to her a package of material (modified spreadsheets, notes, reports etc.) that she can take home and work on in the evening.

Tasks

1. Load Jane's spreadsheet filename **ASS6_KOOL_Q** and improve its general appearance and readability by adding titles and formats as you see fit.

2. Add a column to show the expected closing stock.

3. Your list of closing balances should show up some negative balances. Write a brief informal report for Jane that:

    - Identifies the negative balances

    - Suggests how they might have arisen

    - Discusses their implications

4. Use your closing stock figures to create a column which shows stock turnover figures for each product.

    (Note. You have discussed how to calculate stock turnover with Jane and have agreed that the most appropriate method is to divide the total sales figure for the year by the average of stock held at the beginning and the end of the year.)

5. Jane would like to use the spreadsheet as a basis for quarterly stocktaking. In order to see how viable this is she would like you to create a new version of ASS6_KOOL_Q which provides a list of stock items that the staff can use to enter actual stock levels. Save this new file to floppy disk and print two pages of this spreadsheet as a sample of your proposed stocktaking record.

6. Jane feels that she ought to be able to use the spreadsheet to help her understand the sales pattern in the business. She believes that she has only a limited understanding of the importance of the various lines and would like to get a better feel for what is happening. She is even aware that she does not know which are the right questions to ask.

    In your discussions with Jane you have explained that a spreadsheet is not the best tool for this analysis but you have agreed to try to help.

    It has been decided that your task is to investigate the sales patterns by looking just at the styles from one manufacturer (Hike) and to write a note for Jane that:

    - Provides her with some insight into the sales pattern (for example the relative importance of the childrens' and adults' ranges, the relative importance of mens' and womens' styles and the distribution of sizes)

    - Provides her with some information about which lines she should concentrate on in the future and which she should consider dropping

    - Identifies the problems involved in making a decision to delete a product line on the basis of information presented in the spreadsheet.

Answer to assignment 1:

Broom Riggs

The solution is available in the BPP file **ASS1_BROOM_S** Open the file, select Tools, Options, and then tick the Formulas box in the View tab to see the formulae we used. Other approaches may be equally as valid.

Other points are noted below.

For part (c), you should know how to use whatever anti-virus measures are installed on your PC. You may have a proprietary package such as McAfee or Nortons.

In part (g), to set a 3½ floppy disk to write protect, you should slide the plastic tab to leave the hole visible.

The Page Setup options Landscape and Fit to 1 page wide by 1 page tall should help you complete part (j).

Answer to assignment 2:

Wild Thyme

The solution is available in the BPP file **ASS2_WILD_S**

Open the file, select Tools, Options, and then tick the Formulas box in the View tab to see the formulae we used. Other approaches may be equally as valid.

Also look at the different versions of the sheet on the different worksheets within the file.

Answer to assignment 3:

Island Quay

The solution is available in the BPP file **ASS3_ISLAND_S**

Open the file, select Tools, Options, and then tick the Formulas box in the View tab to see the formulae we used. Other approaches may be equally as valid.

Answer to assignment 4:

Marvels

The solution is available in the BPP file **ASS4_MARVELS_S**

Open the file, select Tools, Options, and then tick the Formulas box in the View tab to see the formulae we used. Other approaches may be equally as valid.

Aspects of the answer requiring further explanation are discussed below.

Task 1

The columns need resizing to accommodate all the information they hold. They should be given headings where they lack them, and these should be emphasised by formatting. It is usual to right align money amounts (the 30, 60, 90 day and Total columns). Most of the text items look best if they are left aligned.

It is useful to bring the monetary columns over next to the Customer names, since it is most likely to be these figures that will change most often and need to be worked on. Hopefully you were careful not to overwrite any information if you did this.

You should also **not leave any blank columns**, because this can affect how data is **sorted**. Refer to our suggested answer in the file ASS4_MARVELS_S to see improvements of this kind.

The sheet should be given a name like **Marvels Ltd – Aged Debtors**. (Our answer, however, names sheets according to the Task that is being answered, for the sake of clarity.)

Task 2

For our coding system we have simply started numbering from 1 upwards. Numbers are shown as six figure numbers (000001) to allow for plenty of flexibility in the future (for instance up to 999,999 accounts!). There are of course many other possible coding systems and any sensible solution is acceptable here.

It is important that you put in your codes before you do any of the sorting of data that is useful for the remainder of this Task. There may be some significance in the order in which customers are entered. We do not know whether there is or not yet, so it is sensible to preserve the original order, at least for now.

We give all the B & Q stores the name 'B & Q DIY Supercentre', since this is the name that recurs most frequently.

'Do It All Ltd' is the most common form, so we have standardised these entries.

'Fads' appears simply as 'Fads' most often so this is the form we use throughout.

Other standards are 'Focus DIY Ltd' (no spaces), 'Great Mills DIY Superstore', 'Homebase Ltd' ('Sainsbury's Homebase' has also been changed to this), 'Homestyle', 'Texas Homecare Ltd', 'Wickes Building Supplies Ltd'.

The above were the accounts we thought requiring editing for consistency of name. There are, however, many names that you may have considered worth noting down for further investigation. There is no one 'right' answer.

We made it easier to pick out possible similar names by sorting the data by name and then using a temporary formula in column O. We did this after **hiding** the intervening rows temporarily – as shown on the following illustration.

	A	B	O	P	Q	R	S	
1	Code	Name						
2	000067	1st Stop D-i-y						
3	000188	A G Direct						
4	000031	A G Stanley Ltd						
5	000169	A S Gill						
6	000210	A S Golding	1					
7	000196	A T D I Y Layzell					=IF(LEFT(B2,4)=LEFT(B1,4),1,"")	
8	000198	Abbasi D I Y						
9	000389	Aber Valley D I Y						
10	000040	Ace Decore Colour & Design Centre						
11	000324	Ace Supply D I Y Ltd	1					
12	000239	Adaptions						
13	000251	Albert Dawson Ltd						
14	000290	Albrion Sales Ltd						
15	000334	Allen Bernard						
16	000407	Allwares						
17	000374	Arnold Laver Ltd						
18	000265	Art & Wood Supplies Do It Yourself						
19	000362	Artorder Ltd						
20	000382	Atlas D I Y Centre						
21	000325	Autopaint International						
22	000166	Avanti Window Systems						
23	000002	B & Q DIY Supercentre						
24	000041	B & Q DIY Supercentre	1					
25	000053	B & Q DIY Supercentre	1					
26	000061	B & Q DIY Supercentre	1					
27	000072	B & Q DIY Supercentre	1					

This extracts the first four characters in one cell (the first four at the LEFT) and compares them with the first four in the cell above. If the characters are identical, a 1 is shown in the equivalent cell in column F; if not nothing is shown.

Duplicates can be found using a similar technique. In this instance we sorted by telephone numbers and then searched for duplicates using =IF(L2=L1,1,"") and so on. You can sum the column first to see if there are any duplicates at all (it will sum to more than 0 if there are).

	A	B	G	L	O	P	Q	R
145	000372	D I Y Electrics	125 Exeter Road	01496 378500				
146	000320	Do-it-yourself Electrics	125 Exeter Road	01496 378500			=IF(L146=L145,1,"")	
147	000326	B & Q DIY Supercentre	Liverton Retail Park	01496 389451				
148	000192	S D I Y Clutton	46 Temple Street	01496 613095				
149	000196	A T D I Y Layzell	107 Temple Street	01496 614379				
150	000278	D I Y At Layzells D I Y Supplies	107 Temple Street	01496 614379	1			
151	000068	Nimmak Security & DIY	Sauchiehall Street	0151 4411914				
152	000008	Do-it-yourself	82 Niddrie Road	0151 5343699				
153	000279	Miller D I Y Supplies	90 Springburn Way	0151 6698443				
154	000173	B & Q DIY Supercentre	21 Legatston Road	0151 7313355				
155	000201	B & Q DIY Supercentre	Shawfield Industrial Estate	0151 7581956				
156	000165	Texas Homecare Ltd	222 Nether Auldhouse Road	0151 7593130				
157	000215	B & Q DIY Supercentre	Strathkelvin Retail Park	0151 8735667				

MEMO

To: Sami Johnswell
From: Accounting Technician
Date: 3 November 20X6

Subject: Duplicate customer accounts

As you know, this week I have been having a close examination of the customer records. One of the matters that has come to light is that there are a number of instances where we appear to have opened two accounts for a single customer.

The instances I found are shown in the following table.

Code	Name	Address 1	Telephone	Balance £
000320	Do-it-yourself Electrics	125 Exeter Road	01496 378500	737.80
000372	D I Y Electrics	125 Exeter Road	01496 378500	1,552.95
				2,290.75
000196	A T D I Y Layzell	107 Temple Street	01496 614379	1,951.60
000278	D I Y At Layzells D I Y Supplies	107 Temple Street	01496 614379	1,029.35
				2,980.95
000090	Milton's Timbers	232 The Broadway	0191 3030377	1,481.55
000350	Milton's Timbers	232 The Broadway	0191 3030377	12.30
				1,493.85
000180	B & Q DIY Supercentre	Larch Drive	0191 9969039	1,862.35
000378	B & Q DIY Supercentre	2 Larch Drive	0191 9969039	71.40
				1,933.75

I trust you will pursue this as you see fit, and advise me of the outcome of any discussions with customers.

In addition, the following customers have identical phone numbers, but different names or addresses. Could we please investigate to establish if these accounts are duplicates.

Code	Name	Address 1	Post Code	Telephone	Balance £
000107	Homebase Ltd	Rookery Way	NW9 6SS	0191 3008600	1,999.20
000244	Texas Homecare Ltd	Colindale Capitol Park	NW9 0EQ	0191 3008600	285.60
					2,284.80
000087	Focus DIY Ltd	Benton Park Road	NE7 7LX	0191 3141744	327.25
000434	Focus DIY Ltd	Unit 1 Westmorland Way	NE1 1AA	0191 3141744	1,541.05
					1,868.30
000214	Maxwells (Sunderland) Ltd	Old Co-op Buildings	NE9 5PJ	0191 5985360	321.30
000225	Maxwells D.I.Y	35 Sheriff High Way	NE9 5PJ	0191 5985360	1,892.10
					2,213.40
000241	Homebase Ltd	Syon Lane	TW7 5BT	0191 9584798	2,600.15
000246	Homebase Ltd	Brentford Capital Interchange	TW8 1XX	0191 9584798	2,142.00
					4,742.15

Task 3

Tutorial note. To generate information for this Task you could either use a Pivot Table (as we do in our answer) or use your spreadsheet's sorting and filtering facilities.

Our Pivot Table was set up very simply (as shown on the following page). We then did further calculations on the same sheet, as reflected in our report.

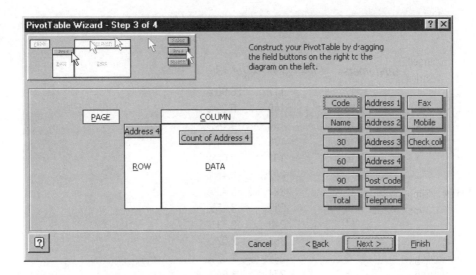

REPORT

To: Charles Davis
From: Accounting Technician
Date: 3 November 20X6

Subject: Geographical sales patterns

1. Introduction

As requested, I have investigated the geographical spread of our customers. My findings are produced below.

2. Findings

The vast majority of out customers are spread throughout the cities of the UK. A total of 105 different towns are represented amongst our 435 customer accounts. In Appendix One I list the top 30 towns, all of which have three customers or more.

We have over five times as many customers in London than in the next best represented city, Bristol. Possibly our product is less well known outside the capital, or possibly there are problems in getting the product to distant locations.

The information suggests that marketing and distribution efforts in the future should concentrate on other major cities, notably Bristol, Leeds, Manchester, Glasgow, Birmingham, Newcastle and Southampton.

Note

The figures provided may be slightly misleading, because it is based on 'postal town' information entered into the customer records. If we look at postcodes we find that there are, for instance, 18 customers with a Birmingham post code, although not all of them have 'Birmingham' in their address.

Appendix 1

Town	Customers	Cumulative	% (of 435)
London	117	117	26.90%
Bristol	23	140	5.29%
Leeds	18	158	4.14%
Manchester	18	176	4.14%
Glasgow	16	192	3.68%
Birmingham	15	207	3.45%
Newcastle Upon Tyne	15	222	3.45%
Southampton	15	237	3.45%
Ipswich	11	248	2.53%
Cardiff	9	257	2.07%
Exeter	9	266	2.07%
Morecambe	8	274	1.84%
Chester	7	281	1.61%
Wrexham	7	288	1.61%
Aberdeen	5	293	1.15%
Eastleigh	5	298	1.15%
Canterbury	4	302	0.92%
Dover	4	306	0.92%
Dundee	4	310	0.92%
Enfield	4	314	0.92%
Exmouth	4	318	0.92%
Gateshead	4	322	0.92%
Newport	4	326	0.92%
Blackpool	3	329	0.69%
Deeside	3	332	0.69%
Fareham	3	335	0.69%
Harwich	3	338	0.69%
Lancaster	3	341	0.69%
Mold	3	344	0.69%
Paisley	3	347	0.69%

END OF REPORT

BPP
PROFESSIONAL EDUCATION

Discrepancies noted in customer address information

Matters to investigate

Code	Name	Address 1	Address 2	Comment
000143	Redcroft	286 Chester Road		No postcode
000250	B & Q DIY Supercentre	Garthdee Road		No postcode
000304	Fairleys Ltd	36-38 Roker Avenue		No postcode

Errors to correct

Code	Name	Address 1	Address 2	Comment
000040	Ace Decore Colour & Design Centre	Unit 8 Clarence Street		Street name should be in Address 2 column
000131	Kemp Bros	High Street		Address 3 and 4, Telephone and fax are in the wrong columns
000215	B & Q DIY Supercentre	Strathkelvin Retail Park		Fax number is nonsense (shown as 151, part of area code). Delete.
000328	Cash-save DIY Ltd	16	6 -176 North Street	Should be 166-176 in Address 1 column
000369	D I Y Discount	62 Old Church St	10	10 is meaningless. Delete.
000381	Focus DIY Ltd	Unit 1 Whistleberry Road		Street name should be in Address 2 column
000392	Home & Garden Supplies	11	5 -117 Penshurst Road	Should be 115 –117 in Address 1 column

Task 4

In our version of the sheet created for Task 4, all the errors found in Task 3 have been posted. Here are the errors.

Code	Name	30	60	90	Original Total	Revised Total	Difference
000028	Rkp Hardware	1052.88	1095.85	5.17	2150.00	2153.90	3.90
000042	Do It All Ltd	843.24	1030.63	339.53	2218.40	2213.40	-5.00
000058	Wasons Paint Paper & D I Y	105.08	73.03	0.39	300.50	178.50	-122.00
000084	Do It All Ltd	67.51	101.27	27.57	916.35	196.35	-720.00
000126	Texas Homecare Ltd	1376.53	1081.56	213.46	2761.55	2671.55	-90.00
000139	Great Mills DIY Superstore	310.55	411.65	3.70	725.09	725.90	0.81
000175	B & Q DIY Supercentre	753.51	723.96	75.48	5112.95	1552.95	-3560.00
000224	M M Patel	923.85	852.79	38.11	184.75	1814.75	1630.00
000241	Homebase Ltd	1169.01	1428.80	2.34	2600.51	2600.15	-0.36
000255	G Langford	507.04	449.64	48.87	1000.00	1005.55	5.55
000284	Decora DIY Superstore	577.41	491.87	0.00	1285.20	1069.28	-215.92
000433	Texas Homecare Ltd	588.24	588.23	55.18	1234.56	1231.65	-2.91
							-3075.93

REPORT

To: Charles Davis
From: Accounting Technician
Date: 3 November 20X6

Subject: Aged debtors analysis

1. Introduction

As requested, I have investigated the current situation regarding money owed to the company and speed of payment. My findings are produced below.

2. Findings

The company is presently owed more than half a million ponds by debtors. An analysis of this total by age gives the following results.

0-30	31-60	61-90	Total
305,618.62	310,756.89	34,880.42	651,255.93
47%	48%	5%	100%

As shown in the table, nearly half of this debt is less than one month old and 95% is less than two months old. According to this analysis there are no amounts that have been outstanding for more than three months, which may be due to such debts being written off.

The relatively good payment record of our debtors should mean the company need have relatively few worries about continuing to be able to finance its overdraft: this record of cash collection should satisfy our bank. However, it would be useful to see information on trends in previous months, to see whether the age of debts has increased.

The largest single total outstanding is £2,975, owed by Homebase in Southampton. However there are eleven other accounts owing more than £2,900, thirteen owing over £2,800 and fourteen owing over £2,700: debts are spread fairly evenly over a range from under £15 up to almost £3,000.

The largest amount outstanding for over 60 days is £544.99 (Emerys Home Improvements, Solihull). Surprisingly only fifteen of the 435 accounts have a nil balance in the over 60 days column. More surprisingly, no customers have a nil balance. This is clearly healthy for business (customers keep on buying) if it is correct, but it is quite unusual.

It is interesting to look at the data if the amounts owed by customers with accounts at more than one branch are amalgamated. A list of customers who then owe more than £5,000 is presented below.

The major DIY stores are the biggest debtors. B & Q stores represent the biggest single debtor, owing 12% of the total amount outstanding, or around £80,000. Homebase come next with 7% (over £45,000). Unfortunately we do not have sales turnover information: it would be interesting to know whether B & Q are significantly our biggest customer (and why, if so) or if they are just the slowest payer amongst big customers. The figures are shown below.

Name	Balance	% of Total
B & Q DIY Supercentre	80622.50	12%
Homebase Ltd	45648.40	7%
Do It All Ltd	26245.45	4%
Great Mills DIY Superstore	19426.75	3%
Texas Homecare Ltd	17850.00	3%
Wickes Building Supplies Ltd	12161.80	2%
Fads	11376.40	2%
Focus DIY Ltd	8692.95	1%
Homestyle	4992.05	1%
Do It Yourself Supplies	4777.85	1%
Magnet Ltd	4527.95	1%
Glyn Web	4266.15	1%

Please contact me if you require clarification or further information.

Tutorial note. You could use sorting and filtering to derive the above information or else use a Pivot Table. Here is how the information about DIY chain stores was generated.

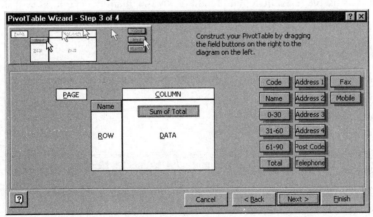

The data in the Pivot Table then had to be selected and sorted, and an additional percentage column was calculated.

Answer to assignment 5:

Harry Alexander

The solution is available in the BPP file **ASS5_HARRY_S**

Open the file, select Tools, Options, and then tick the Formulas box in the View tab to see the formulae we used. Other approaches may be equally as valid.

Aspects of the answer requiring further explanation are discussed below.

Task 1

If you look at our solution in the file ASS5_HARRY_S, you will see that we entered the data into columns A to E of a separate sheet.

The employee numbers can be checked by visual inspection very easily. The materials codes are much more difficult to check. In our answer we have extracted the letters and numbers using the formulae =LEFT(A1,2) in column G, =RIGHT(A1,4) in column H, and =VALUE(H2) in column I. This at least allows you to calculate a total of the four digit numbers in the materials codes. An alternative way of ensuring accuracy might have been to copy the Materials code column, sort it, and then delete duplicates.

Task 2

Here is the answer. The totals are shown in Row 422 of our answer.

	£
Total materials cost	47,467.33
Total labour cost	35,364.80
	82,832.13

The best way to do this is to use the **LOOKUP** function in columns E and I. (A slower alternative would be to enter the data line by line, after sorting it by materials code.)

The formulae we use refer to the sheet Task 1 (Lookup) in which we have entered the cost and rate data (see the solution to Task 1). They look up the relevant cost and multiply by the quantity in column D or the hours in column H.

Column E   =D2*LOOKUP(C2,'Task 1 (Lookup)'!$A$1:$B$23)

Column I=H2*LOOKUP(F2,'Task 1 (Lookup)'!$D$1:$E$24)

Make sure you understand this because it is a very useful feature. (If necessary, consult Help in Excel for more details on this function.)

Task 3

> **Tutorial note**. You could have used Pivot Tables to complete this task, constructing separate Pivot Tables for materials costs and labour costs. Alternatively you can use sorting or filters to extract and sum the information from the main table and successively paste the totals for each job into another sheet. Note that a chart of the data is very useful.

REPORT

To: Production Manager
From: Accounting Technician
Date: 5 November 20X4

Subject: Job costs, October 20X4

Job costs for the month may be summarised as follows. All costs are shown in £'s.

	By job				*By total cost*		
Job	*Total cost*	*Materials cost*	*Labour cost*	*Job*	*Total cost*	*Materials cost*	*Labour cost*
724	7,696.35	3,979.65	3,716.70	728	10,112.00	4,809.50	5,302.50
725	7,949.35	5,308.25	2,641.10	732	9,789.85	5,398.15	4,391.70
726	6,763.83	3,580.53	3,183.30	731	9,125.20	5,477.10	3,648.10
727	8,509.91	4,287.41	4,222.50	733	8,900.11	4,586.71	4,313.40
728	10,112.00	4,809.50	5,302.50	727	8,509.91	4,287.41	4,222.50
729	7,507.32	5,763.82	1,743.50	725	7,949.35	5,308.25	2,641.10
730	6,478.21	4,276.21	2,202.00	724	7,696.35	3,979.65	3,716.70
731	9,125.20	5,477.10	3,648.10	729	7,507.32	5,763.82	1,743.50
732	9,789.85	5,398.15	4,391.70	726	6,763.83	3,580.53	3,183.30
733	8,900.11	4,586.71	4,313.40	730	6,478.21	4,276.21	2,202.00
	82,832.13	47,467.33	35,364.80		82,832.13	47,467.33	35,364.80

Job 728 was the most expensive, costing over £10,000 to complete, while Job 730, done at a cost of around £6,500, was the least expensive.

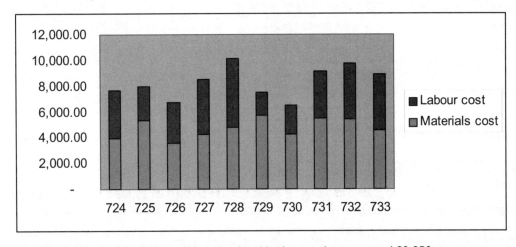

The average cost for all of the ten jobs completed in the month was around £8,250.

A breakdown of costs into labour and materials totals reveals certain matters that may be worthy of further investigation. Most jobs have a materials cost that is only slightly higher than the labour cost, but the following jobs depart from this trend.

(a) Job 729 cost over £5,750 in materials but less than £1,750 in labour.
(b) Job 725 was nearly £3,000 more expensive in terms of materials than labour.
(c) Jobs 730 and 731 were around £2,000 more expensive in terms of materials than labour.
(d) Job 728 cost around £500 more in labour than it did in materials.

Notes and queries for personal use

1   Which jobs were accepted at the standard price of £10,000 and which not? The company will make a loss on job 728, and only a relatively small profit on job 732. If all jobs are priced at £10,000 a mark up of a third is only achieved on three out of ten (726, 729, 730).

2   Can jobs be identified in advance as being particularly labour intensive or materials intensive? If they could be categorised at the outset as, say 'L' jobs for labour intensive, or 'M' jobs for materials intensive, this might be useful, both for planning in the personnel and purchasing departments, and for later analysis.

3   How is work allocated between staff? Some staff are paid considerably more than others, and this may have a bearing on costs incurred. On the other hand, salaries/wages may be fixed costs.

4   Do labour and materials costs change from month to month? If not this data could be incorporated permanently into a spreadsheet model rather than having to be re-entered and carefully checked each time.

5   Can I be sure that all the figures for quantities and hours have been entered accurately?

Tutorial note. Many points could be made here. Marks should be awarded for valid comments of any kind. The spreadsheet upon which the information provided in the report is based will be found in the BPP file ASS5_HARRY_S. This was originally generated using Pivot Tables for Materials cost and then again for Labour cost (see the sheet Task 3 (Pivot) for a sample based on cells **B1 to E421 only** of the main spreadsheet).

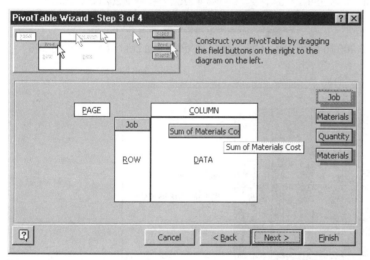

The data from the Pivot Tables was copied and pasted into another sheet, summed, and then copied again and sorted by total cost. The final sheet is reproduced below in 'formula' format.

	A	B	C	D	E	F	G	H	I	J
1	Job	Total cost	Materials cost	Labour cost			Job	Total cost	Materials cost	Labour cost
2	724	=SUM(C2:D2)	3979.65	3716.7			728	=SUM(I2:J2)	4809.5	5302.5
3	725	=SUM(C3:D3)	5308.25	2641.1			732	=SUM(I3:J3)	5398.15	4391.7
4	726	=SUM(C4:D4)	3580.53	3183.3			731	=SUM(I4:J4)	5477.1	3648.1
5	727	=SUM(C5:D5)	4287.41	4222.5			733	=SUM(I5:J5)	4586.71	4313.4
6	728	=SUM(C6:D6)	4809.5	5302.5			727	=SUM(I6:J6)	4287.41	4222.5
7	729	=SUM(C7:D7)	5763.82	1743.5			725	=SUM(I7:J7)	5308.25	2641.1
8	730	=SUM(C8:D8)	4276.21	2202			724	=SUM(I8:J8)	3979.65	3716.7
9	731	=SUM(C9:D9)	5477.1	3648.1			729	=SUM(I9:J9)	5763.82	1743.5
10	732	=SUM(C10:D10)	5398.15	4391.7			726	=SUM(I10:J10)	3580.53	3183.3
11	733	=SUM(C11:D11)	4586.71	4313.4			730	=SUM(I11:J11)	4276.21	2202
12		=SUM(B2:B11)	=SUM(C2:C11)	=SUM(D2:D11)				=SUM(H2:H11)	=SUM(I2:I11)	=SUM(J2:J11)
13										
14		Maximum	Job 728	=MAX(B2:B11)						
15		Minimum	Job 730	=MIN(B2:B11)						
16		Average	of all jobs	=AVERAGE(B2:B11)						

The chart is produced by selecting the Materials cost and Labour cost data and specifying the Job number data as the Category X axis labels.

Task 4

The material TP7325 data can be extracted by sorting the main spreadsheet on the relevant column.

REPORT

To: Production Manager
From: Accounting Technician
Date: 5 November 20X4

Subject: Materials usage, October 20X4

Jobs 718 and 730

As requested, the table below shows a summary of the differences in material usage between Job 718 and Job 730.

Material	718	730	Difference
AH8317	7	7	0
BX3662	36	36	0
CZ8997	40	42	2
DN9569	22	60	38
ED2677	80	79	-1
FW4100	42		-42
GY2898			0
HU2871	5	5	0
JV7549	62	65	3
KM6315	70	72	2
LJ1234	75	75	0
MT9908	40	41	1
NG7732	60	59	-1
PF6023	124	113	-11
QE2207	10	12	2
RK3583	50	57	7
TP7325			0
UQ7049	80	82	2
VA1662		42	42
WL5592	34	34	0
XC5229			0
YR8218	47	47	0
ZB2520	149	149	0
	1033	1077	44

The following points may be noted.

(a)   Job 730 used more materials overall than job 718, though not significantly more so. This is largely accounted for by the fact that Job 730 used 38 more units of DN9569 than Job 718.

(b)   Materials FW4100 and VA1662 may be interchangeable: Job 718 used 42 units of FW4100 while Job 730 used none. Job 730 used 42 units of VA1662 while Job 718 used none.

(c)   Materials GY2898, TP7325 and XC5229 were not used by either job.

(d)   All other differences are negligible.

Material TP7325

Usage of material TP7325 was distributed between jobs as follows.

Job	Total
724	48
725	37
726	47
727	49
728	97
729	14
731	50
732	44
733	91
Total	**477**

The average amount used was 53 units, although this was distorted by two much higher values (Jobs 728 and 733), and one much lower value (Job 729). If this data is removed the average is about 46 units, slightly below your expectations. However, with the exceptions noted, usage was broadly the same across all Jobs.

Overall, usage was down in October 20X4 from 520 units in September to 477 in October. This is perhaps because material TP7325 was not used for Job 730 at all, according to issue note records.

Task 5

NOTE

To: Production Manager
From: Accounting Technician
Date: 5 November 20X4

Subject: Labour hours, October 20X4

Job 728 took longest, at 585 hours, while job 729 took the least time, at less than half of this (221 hours). A full analysis of jobs in order of time spent is shown below.

Job	Hours
728	585
732	473
733	448
727	439
724	427
731	368
725	336
726	327
730	240
729	221

The longest time spent by a single employee on one job was 89 hours, taken by employee P014 on Job 729. All employees worked 184 hours during the month apart from employees P001, P023 and P024, none of whom appear to have worked on jobs at all during the month.

> **Tutorial note**. The illustration below shows how the data required for this answer might be derived by a combination of a pivot table and simple formulae and sorting.

	A	B	C	D	E	F	G	H	I	J	K	L	M	N
1	Sum of Labour hours	Job											Job	Time
2	Employee	724	725	726	727	728	729	730	731	732	733	Grand Total	=F$2	=F$24
3	P002			77		67			40			184	=J$2	=J$24
4	P003			24		40			37		83	184	=K$2	=K$24
5	P004	42			77			31	34			184	=E$2	=E$24
6	P005	68			61	55						184	=B$2	=B$24
7	P006	34		29				79	42			184	=I$2	=I$24
8	P007				34		71				79	184	=C$2	=C$24
9	P008	11	62	28	14		10	17		42		184	=D$2	=D$24
10	P009	10	49		16			30		35	44	184	=H$2	=H$24
11	P010			28	24	30		58			44	184	=G$2	=G$24
12	P011	7	12			60	12		38	55		184		
13	P012				62	38	72		12			184		
14	P013	50		71				7		56		184		
15	P014			26		6	89				63	184		
16	P015		15		39	19	38			12	61	184		
17	P016			43	47	83			11			184		
18	P017		38	1					71		74	184		
19	P018	17			53		51	63				184		
20	P019	58	32			42	31	21				184		
21	P020	66		12	66			10	30			184		
22	P021	46			55		19		64			184		
23	P022	84	62		24		14					184		
24	Grand Total	427	336	327	439	585	221	240	368	473	448	3864		
25														
26	Longest	=MAX(B24:K24)												
27	Shortest	=MIN(B24:K24)												
28	Average	=AVERAGE(B24:K24)												
29	Longest E'ee time	=MAX(B3:K23)												

Sort

Sort by
[Time] ○ Ascending ● Descending

Then by
[ ] ● Ascending ○ Descending

Then by
[ ] ● Ascending ○ Descending

My list has
● Header row   ○ No header row

Options...   OK   Cancel

Answer to assignment 6:
KoolFoot

The solution is available in the BPP file **ASS6_KOOL_S**

Open the file, select Tools, Options, and then tick the Formulas box in the View tab to see the formulae we used. Other approaches may be equally as valid.

Aspects of the answer requiring further explanation are discussed below.

Task 1

You should have provided some form of heading for the spreadsheet to explain its purpose, and tidied up the column headings and aligned them with the data.

Your spreadsheet should look something like this.

	A	B	C	D	E	F	G	H	I
1					Stocklist as at 28th March				
2									
3	Count	Maker	Style	B/M/G/W	Size	Product	Opening	Sales	Deliveries
4						Code	Stock		
5	1	H	1	B	26	H1B26	1	0	1
6	2	H	1	B	27	H1B27	1	1	1
7	3	H	1	B	28	H1B28	1	1	1
8	4	H	1	B	29	H1B29	2	2	2
9	5	H	1	B	30	H1B30	0	2	2
10	6	H	1	B	31	H1B31	2	1	1
11	7	H	1	B	32	H1B32	0	1	1
12	8	H	1	B	33	H1B33	1	2	2
13	9	H	1	B	34	H1B34	0	1	1
14	10	H	1	B	35	H1B35	2	3	3
15	11	H	1	B	36	H1B36	0	2	2

The extra column showing each **Product Code** in a single cell (which is potentially useful for any further analysis of the data) can be generated by using the formula =B3&C3&D3&E3.

Task 2

The formula to use in cell J5 (if your spreadsheet is laid out like ours) is =G5-H5+I5. You can then fill down with the mouse to complete the other rows.

	A	B	C	D	E	F	G	H	I	J
1					Stocklist as at 28th March					
2										
3	Count	Maker	Style	B/M/G/W	Size	Product	Opening	Sales	Deliveries	Closing
4						Code	Stock			Stock
5	1	H	1	B	26	H1B26	1	0	1	=G5-H5+I5
6	2	H	1	B	27	H1B27	1	1	1	1
7	3	H	1	B	28	H1B28	1	1	1	1
8	4	H	1	B	29	H1B29	2	2	2	2

If your first row is correct, all the others should be too. However, if you wish to check every row of your own answer you can copy the closing stock column from our answer, paste it in into your spreadsheet (using the **Paste Special ... Values** option) and then subtract your column from ours in the next column. The answer should be zero for each line unless you have made an error, so the column as a whole should sum to zero.

Task 3

> **Tutorial note**. In Excel you can use the **Data ... Filter ... Auto Filter** to identify negative balances, and copy and paste them into a new spreadsheet once you have found them. There are only three, as shown in our answer below.
>
> Alternatively, but just as effectively, you could **Sort** the data in ascending numerical order, on the **Closing Stock** column.
>
> Alternatively you could use a formula in another column such as =IF(J5<0,"Error","OK") and then fill down the other rows. This makes the negative balances stand out more as you scroll through the list. To be sure you had found them all you could do a **Find** for "Error".

REPORT

To: Jane Jones
From: Accounting Technician
Date: 31 March 20X5

Negative Stock Balances

An analysis of your stock records spreadsheet reveals that the following products have negative values for stock as at 28 March 20X5. A negative balance is, of course, impossible because we are dealing with physical items.

Count	Maker	Style	B/M/G/W	Size	Product Code	Opening Stock	Sales	Deliveries	Closing Stock
25	H	1	G	32	H1G32	0	2	1	-1
88	H	7	G	26	H7G26	0	11	10	-1
161	0	5	G	29	05G29	0	11	10	-1

Negative Stock balances

These errors may have arisen for a number of reasons.

    (a)   Errors in recording the opening stock figure.
    (b)   Errors in recording sales.
    (c)   Errors recording delivery quantities.
    (d)   Because sales of other products have been incorrectly allocated to these products.
    (e)   The records may have been deliberately altered, for instance in an attempt to cover up theft of stock.

The only obvious pattern to the errors discovered so far is that each item with a negative balance is a girl's shoe. It may be worth considering whether records for these have been dealt with differently (for instance entered by a different person) from other shoes.

Although errors have only been definitely identified in three product records (less than 1% of the total) the existence of three clear errors implies that there may be further errors which have not yet been detected. For instance the spreadsheet may show closing stock for an item as 4, whereas in reality there are 3 or 5 items in stock. Such a discrepancy could arise for any of the reasons stated above.

Only a full, thorough count of physical stock will reveal the extent of such errors. I strongly recommend that such a count is made as soon as possible. Meanwhile records of sales and deliveries for the three items identified above should be investigated to see if the errors can be traced.

Task 4

You are instructed to calculate stock turnover as Sales/(Opening Stock + Closing Stock/2). This is therefore exactly what you should do, even though you may feel that it is not completely appropriate.

To avoid a "Divide by 0" error, we have included an **if** statement in our answer, as follows.

=IF((J5+G5)/2=0,"",(H5/((J5+G5)/2)))

This gives blank cells where opening and closing stock is zero. In such cases stock turnover is **really** either 1.00 (if there was no opening or closing stock and all deliveries have been sold: eg item H1B30) or 0.00 (if the item has not been in stock, sold or delivered all year eg item H5W44). It is merely coincidence that stocks were nil on the opening and closing days. A better formula might be =IF((J5+G5)/2=0,(H5/I5),(H5/((J5+G5)/2))).

Score bonus marks if you pointed this out in your answer. However, you **must** use the calculation method prescribed in the instructions. If you simply used a formula like =H5/((J5+G5)/2) you should get full marks.

The first few lines of our answer are shown on the following page. The formula is shown in cell K5. We have formatted column K to show figures to 2 decimal places.

	A	B	C	D	E	F	G	H	I	J	K
1						Stocklist as at 28th March					
2											
3	Count	Maker	Style	B/M/G/W	Size	Product Code	Opening Stock	Sales	Deliveries	Closing Stock	Stock Turnover
5	1	H	1	B	26	H1B26	1	0	1	2	=IF((J5+G5)/2=0,"",(H5/((J5+G5)/2)))
6	2	H	1	B	27	H1B27	1	1	1	1	1.00
7	3	H	1	B	28	H1B28	1	1	1	1	1.00
8	4	H	1	B	29	H1B29	2	2	2	2	1.00
9	5	H	1	B	30	H1B30	0	2	2	0	
10	6	H	1	B	31	H1B31	2	1	1	2	0.50
11	7	H	1	B	32	H1B32	0	1	1	0	
12	8	H	1	B	33	H1B33	1	2	2	1	2.00
13	9	H	1	B	34	H1B34	0	1	1	0	
14	10	H	1	B	35	H1B35	2	3	3	2	1.50
15	11	H	1	B	36	H1B36	0	2	2	0	
16	12	H	1	B	37	H1B37	1	2	3	2	1.33
17	13	H	1	M	38	H1M38	0	5	5	0	
18	14	H	1	M	40	H1M40	0	6	10	4	3.00
19	15	H	1	M	42	H1M42	1	19	20	2	12.67
20	16	H	1	M	44	H1M44	1	15	20	6	4.29
21	17	H	1	M	46	H1M46	0	5	5	0	
22	18	H	1	M	48	H1M48	1	11	10	0	22.00
23	19	H	1	G	26	H1G26	0	2	2	0	
24	20	H	1	G	27	H1G27	1	2	3	2	1.33
25	21	H	1	G	28	H1G28	1	2	2	1	2.00
26	22	H	1	G	29	H1G29	1	2	3	2	1.33
27	23	H	1	G	30	H1G30	1	1	1	1	1.00
28	24	H	1	G	31	H1G31	1	1	2	2	0.67
29	25	H	1	G	32	H1G32	0	2	1	-1	-4.00
30	26	H	1	W	34	H1W34	1	4	5	2	2.67

Task 5

The first two pages of our solution follow, shown as they would appear when printed out. Note the following points.

(a) The only information needed to allow the stock take to be completed is the product code. Balances **should not** be included because counters might then be tempted to enter the same figure as shown in the records rather than doing a proper count.

(b) A space should be provided for the person who completed each sheet to enter their name and the date.

(c) Space for entry of numbers and comments should be more than adequate to encourage clear handwriting. (We use a row height of 36.)

(d) Headings should be repeated at the top of each page (for instance in Excel use **Page Setup ... Sheet ... Rows to repeat at top**).

(e) Each page should have an indication of its page number and the total number of pages ("Page 1 of 27" in our example). You can set up the spreadsheet to include this information automatically when printed out, for instance using the **Page Setup ... Header Footer** options.

121

Stocktake List

Date _____

Completed by _____

Product Code	Count	Comments
H1B26		
H1B27		
H1B28		
H1B29		
H1B30		
H1B31		
H1B32		
H1B33		
H1B34		
H1B35		
H1B36		
H1B37		

Page 1 of 27

Stocktake List

Date _____

Completed by _____

Product Code	Count	Comments
H1M38		
H1M40		
H1M42		
H1M44		
H1M46		
H1M48		
H1G26		
H1G27		
H1G28		
H1G29		
H1G30		
H1G31		

Page 2 of 27

Task 6

The following patterns emerge from an analysis of the sales data for Hike shoes.

Sales by sex and age

Boys shoes	83
Girls shoes	140
Men's shoes	597
Women's shoes	<u>279</u>
Total sales of Hike shoes	1,099

Comment. Adult shoe sales make up more than three quarters of the total. More than twice as many men's shoes are sold as women's shoes. However, more girl's shoes are sold than boy's shoes.

It may be worth considering ceasing to sell children's shoes, and giving the shop space freed to increase the range of adult shoes sold. Alternatively, it may be worth considering stocking cheaper children's shoes, as parents may be reluctant to pay premium prices for high quality shoes that their children may quickly outgrow.

It is also necessary to consider whether dropping children's shoes may have a knock-on effect on sales of adult shoes. Young customers will of course get older, and it may be worth starting to build up customer loyalty at an early age. Some adult customers may wish to take advantage of the fact that they can currently buy shoes for all the family in one shop.

Sales by size, and by sex and age

Size	Sales	Sex/Age	Sales
26	23	B	3
		G	20
27	25	B	5
		G	20
28	20	B	3
		G	17
29	28	B	6
		G	22
30	27	B	7
		G	20
31	26	B	7
		G	19
32	27	B	5
		G	22
33	8	B	8
34	35	B	7
		W	28
35	12	B	12
36	60	B	11
		W	49
37	9	B	9
38	152	M	54
		W	98
40	138	M	72
		W	66
42	209	M	183
		W	26
44	143	M	131
		W	12
46	54	M	54
48	103	M	103

Sales in order of size		
M	42	183
M	44	131
M	48	103
W	38	98
M	40	72
W	40	66
M	38	54
M	46	54
W	36	49
W	34	28
W	42	26
G	29	22
G	32	22
G	26	20
G	27	20
G	30	20
G	31	19
G	28	17
B	35	12
W	44	12
B	36	11
B	37	9
B	33	8
B	30	7
B	31	7
B	34	7
B	29	6
B	27	5
B	32	5
B	26	3
B	28	3

Comment: Most men take a shoe size that is close to 42. Most women take a shoe size that is close to 38. Children's shoes sell in about the same numbers for each size. Stocks of the most common sizes should be maintained at a higher level than for other sizes.

Sales by style

Style 8 (M)	324
Style 6 (M)	212
Style 7 (G/W)	177
Style 1 (B/G/M/W)	133
Style 9 (G/W)	84
Style 2 (G/W)	75
Style 3 (B)	37
Style 5 (G/W)	29
Style 4 (B)	28
Total	1,099

Comment

Styles 8 and 6 are the most popular men's styles. Style 7 is the most popular girl's/ women's style. Style 1 is popular as it appears to be suitable for both sexes and across all ages, whereas style 3, for instance, is only available for boys.

It may be worth considering dropping styles 3, 4 and 5. However, styles 3 and 4 combined make up the majority of sales of boy's shoes.

Products H1B26 (a very small boy's shoe) and H5W44 (a very large women's shoe) have nil sales.

Much of the above information could have been obtained from a pivot table. The pivot table could have been created as follows.

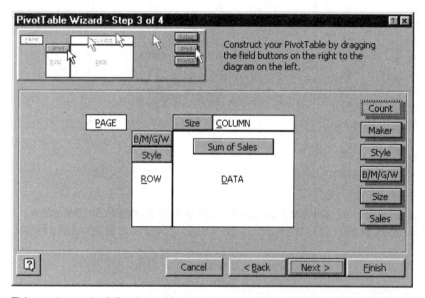

This produces the following table (also included in the BPP file **ASS6_KOOL_S**).

	A	B	C	D	E	F	G	H	I	J	K	L	M	N	O	P	Q	R	S	T	U
1	Sum of Sales		Size																		
2	B/M/G/W	Style	26	27	28	29	30	31	32	33	34	35	36	37	38	40	42	44	46	48	Grand Total
3	B	1	0	1	1	2	2	1	1	2	1	3	2	2							18
4		3	2	2	1	3	3	3	2	3	4	5	5	4							37
5		4	1	2	1	1	2	3	2	3	2	4	4	3							28
6	B Total		3	5	3	6	7	7	5	8	7	12	11	9							83
7	G	1	2	2	2	2	1	1	2												12
8		2	3	4	3	4	4	4	3												25
9		5	1	1	1	2	1	1	2												9
10		7	11	10	8	10	10	9	11												69
11		9	3	3	3	4	4	4	4												25
12	G Total		20	20	17	22	20	19	22												140
13	M	1													5	6	19	15	5	11	61
14		6													20	29	52	51	18	42	212
15		8													29	37	112	65	31	50	324
16	M Total														54	72	183	131	54	103	597
17	W	1								4		8		13	12	3	2			42
18		2								5		9		18	12	4	2			50
19		5								1		4		8	5	2	0			20
20		7								12		20		35	25	10	6			108
21		9								6		8		24	12	7	2			59
22	W Total									28		49		98	66	26	12			279
23	Grand Total		23	25	20	28	27	26	27	8	35	12	60	9	152	138	209	143	54	103	1099

If you did not use the pivot table feature, an alternative approach would have been to extract the following data onto a separate sheet and sort it in a variety of ways. One possible approach is shown below.

	A	B	C	D	E	F
1	Count	Maker	Style	B/M/G/W	Size	Sales
2	1	H	1	B	26	0
3	2	H	1	B	27	1
4	3	H	1	B	28	1
5	4	H	1	B	29	2
6	5	H	1	B	30	2
7	6	H	1	B	31	1
8	7	H	1	B	32	1
9	8	H	1	B	33	2

AAT Order

To BPP Professional Education, Aldine Place, London W12 8AW
Tel: 020 8740 2211. Fax: 020 8740 1184
E-mail: Publishing@bpp.com Web:www.bpp.com

Mr/Mrs/Ms (Full name) _____
Daytime delivery address _____
Postcode _____
Daytime Tel _____
E-mail _____

	5/05 Texts	5/05 Kits	Special offer	8/05 Passcards	Success CDs
FOUNDATION (£14.95 except as indicated)				Foundation	
Units 1 & 2 Receipts and Payments	☐		Foundation Sage Bookeeping and Excel Spreadsheets CD-ROM free if ordering all Foundation Text and Kits, including Units 21 and 22/23 ☐	£6.95 ☐	£14.95 ☐
Unit 3 Ledger Balances and Initial Trial Balance	☐ (Combined Text & Kit)				
Unit 4 Supplying Information for Mgmt Control	☐ (Combined Text & Kit)				
Unit 21 Working with Computers (£9.95)	☐				
Unit 22/23 Healthy Workplace/Personal Effectiveness (£9.95)	☐				
Sage and Excel for Foundation (Workbook with CD-ROM £9.95)	☐				
INTERMEDIATE (£9.95 except as indicated)					
Unit 5 Financial Records and Accounts (for 06/06 exams)	☐	☐		£5.95 ☐	£14.95 ☐
Unit 6/7 Costs and Reports (Combined Text £14.95)	☐			£5.95 ☐	
Unit 6 Costs and Revenues		☐			£14.95 ☐
Unit 7 Reports and Returns		☐			
TECHNICIAN (£9.95 except as indicated)					
Unit 8/9 Core Managing Performance and Controlling Resources	☐	☐		£5.95 ☐	£14.95 ☐
Spreadsheets for Technician (Workbook with CD-ROM)	☐		Spreadsheets for Technicians CD-ROM free if take Unit 8/9 Text and Kit ☐		
Unit 10 Core Managing Systems and People (£14.95)	☐ (Combined Text & Kit)			£5.95 ☐	£14.95 ☐
Unit 11 Option Financial Statements (A/c Practice) (for 06/06 exams)	☐	☐		£5.95 ☐	
Unit 12 Option Financial Statements (Central Govnmt)	☐	☐		£5.95 ☐	
Unit 15 Option Cash Management and Credit Control	☐	☐		£5.95 ☐	
Unit 17 Option Implementing Audit Procedures	☐	☐		£5.95 ☐	
Unit 18 Option Business Tax FA05 (8/05) (£14.95)	☐ (Combined Text & Kit)			£5.95 ☐	
Unit 19 Option Personal Tax FA05 (8/05) (£14.95)	☐ (Combined Text & Kit)			£5.95 ☐	
INTERMEDIATE 2004 (£9.95 except as indicated)					
Unit 5 Financial Records and Accounts (for 12/05 exams)	☐	☐		£5.95 ☐	
TECHNICIAN 2004 (£9.95 except as indicated)					
Unit 11 Option Financial Statements (A/c Practice) (for 12/05 exams)	☐			£5.95 ☐	
Unit 18 Option Business Tax FA04 (8/04)	☐ (Combined Text & Kit)			£5.95 ☐	
Unit 19 Option Personal Tax FA04 (8/04)	☐ (Combined Text & Kit)			£5.95 ☐	
SUBTOTAL	£	£	£	£	£

TOTAL FOR PRODUCTS £ ☐

POSTAGE & PACKING

Texts/Kits	First	Each extra	
UK	£3.00	£3.00	£ ☐
Europe*	£6.00	£4.00	£ ☐
Rest of world	£20.00	£10.00	£ ☐
Passcards			
UK	£2.00	£1.00	£ ☐
Europe*	£3.00	£2.00	£ ☐
Rest of world	£8.00	£8.00	£ ☐
Success CDs			
UK	£2.00	£1.00	£ ☐
Europe*	£3.00	£2.00	£ ☐
Rest of world	£8.00	£8.00	£ ☐

TOTAL FOR POSTAGE & PACKING £ ☐
(Max £12 Texts/Kits/Passcards - deliveries in UK)

Grand Total (Cheques to *BPP Professional Education*)
I enclose a cheque for (incl. Postage) £ ☐
Or charge to Access/Visa/Switch
Card Number ☐☐☐☐ ☐☐☐☐ ☐☐☐☐ ☐☐☐☐
CV2 No ☐☐☐ last 3 digits on signature strip
Expiry date ☐☐☐☐ Start Date ☐☐☐☐
Issue Number (Switch Only) ☐☐
Signature _____

We aim to deliver to all UK addresses inside 5 working days; a signature will be required. Orders to all EU addresses should be delivered within 6 working days. All other orders to overseas addresses should be delivered within 8 working days. * Europe includes the Republic of Ireland and the Channel Islands.

See overleaf for information on other
BPP products and how to order

AAT Order

To BPP Professional Education, Aldine Place, London W12 8AW
Tel: 020 8740 2211. Fax: 020 8740 1184
E-mail: Publishing@bpp.com Web:www.bpp.com

Mr/Mrs/Ms (Full name) _____
Daytime delivery address _____
_____ Postcode _____
Daytime Tel _____ E-mail _____

TOTAL FOR PRODUCTS £ [ ]

POSTAGE & PACKING

Texts/Kits	First	Each extra	
UK	£3.00	£3.00	£ [ ]
Europe*	£6.00	£4.00	£ [ ]
Rest of world	£20.00	£10.00	£ [ ]
Passcards			
UK	£2.00	£1.00	£ [ ]
Europe*	£3.00	£2.00	£ [ ]
Rest of world	£8.00	£8.00	£ [ ]
Tapes			
UK	£2.00	£1.00	£ [ ]
Europe*	£3.00	£2.00	£ [ ]
Rest of world	£8.00	£8.00	£ [ ]

TOTAL FOR POSTAGE & PACKING £ [ ]
(Max £12 Texts/Kits/Passcards - deliveries in UK)

Grand Total (Cheques to *BPP Professional Education*)

I enclose a cheque for (incl. Postage) £ [ ]
Or charge to Access/Visa/Switch
Card Number [ ] CV2 No [ ] last 3 digits on signature strip

Expiry date _____ Start Date _____

Issue Number (Switch Only) _____

Signature _____

OTHER MATERIAL FOR AAT STUDENTS

	8/04 Texts	6/04 Text	3/03 Text	3/04 Text

FOUNDATION (£5.95)
Basic Maths and English ☐

COMPUTER BASED TRAINING
AAT Bookkeeping Certificate (CD-ROM plus manual) £130 ☐

INTERMEDIATE (£5.95)
Basic Bookkeeping (for students exempt from Foundation) ☐
Business Maths and English ☐
(higher level Maths and English, also useful for ACCA/CIMA) £9.95

FOR ALL STUDENTS (£5.95)
Building Your Portfolio (old standards) ☐
Building Your Portfolio (2003 standards) ☐
Basic Costing ☐

AAT PAYROLL

Finance Act 2005 8/05	**Finance Act 2004** 8/04
December 2005 and June 2006 assessments	June 2005 exams only

Special offer
Take Text and Kit together £44.95 ☐

Special offer
Take Text and Kit together £44.95 ☐

LEVEL 2 Text (£29.95)	☐	☐
LEVEL 2 Kit (£19.95)	☐	☐

For assessments in 2006 £44.95 ☐

For assessments in 2005 £44.95 ☐

LEVEL 3 Text (£29.95)	☐	☐
LEVEL 3 Kit (£19.95)	☐	☐
SUBTOTAL	£ [ ]	£ [ ]

We aim to deliver to all UK addresses inside 5 working days; a signature will be required. Orders to all EU addresses should be delivered within 6 working days. All other orders to overseas addresses should be delivered within 8 working days. * Europe includes the Republic of Ireland and the Channel Islands.

Review Form & Free Prize Draw – Excel Exercises for Technician (4/05)

All original review forms from the entire BPP range, completed with genuine comments, will be entered into one of two draws on 31 January 2006 and 31 July 2006. The names on the first four forms picked out on each occasion will be sent a cheque for £50.

Name: _____   Address: _____

_____

_____

How have you used this Workbook?
(Tick one box only)

☐ Home study (book only)

☐ On a course: college _____

☐ With 'correspondence' package

☐ Other _____

Why did you decide to purchase this Workbook? *(Tick one box only)*

☐ Have used BPP Texts/Kits in the past

☐ Recommendation by friend/colleague

☐ Recommendation by a lecturer at college

☐ Saw advertising

☐ Other _____

During the past six months do you recall seeing/receiving any of the following?
(Tick as many boxes as are relevant)

☐ Our advertisement in *Accounting Technician* magazine

☐ Our advertisement in *Pass*

☐ Our brochure with a letter through the post

Which (if any) aspects of our advertising do you find useful?
(Tick as many boxes as are relevant)

☐ Prices and publication dates of new editions

☐ Information on Interactive Text content

☐ Facility to order books off-the-page

☐ None of the above

Have you used other BPP Texts and Kits?   ☐ Yes   ☐ No

Your ratings, comments and suggestions would be appreciated on the following areas

	Very useful	Useful	Not useful
Files on CD	☐	☐	☐
Activities and answers	☐	☐	☐
Assignments and answers	☐	☐	☐

	Excellent	Good	Adequate	Poor
Overall opinion of this Workbook	☐	☐	☐	☐

Do you intend to continue using BPP products?   ☐ Yes   ☐ No

The BPP author of this edition can be e-mailed at: barrywalsh@bpp.com

Please return this form to Janice Ross, BPP Professional Education, FREEPOST, London W12 8BR

Please note any further comments and suggestions/errors on the reverse of this page.

Review Form & Free Prize Draw (continued)

Please note any further comments and suggestions/errors below

Free Prize Draw Rules

1   Closing date for 31 January 2006 draw is 31 December 2005. Closing date for 31 July 2006 draw is 30 June 2006.

2   Restricted to entries with UK and Eire addresses only. BPP employees, their families and business associates are excluded.

3   No purchase necessary. Entry forms are available upon request from BPP Professional Education. No more than one entry per title, per person. Draw restricted to persons aged 16 and over.

4   Winners will be notified by post and receive their cheques not later than 6 weeks after the relevant draw date.

5   The decision of the promoter in all matters is final and binding. No correspondence will be entered into.